Lecture Notes in Artificial Intelligence 597

Subseries of Lecture Notes in Computer Science
Edited by J. Siekmann

Lecture Notes in Computer Science
Edited by G. Goos and J. Hartmanis

H. W. Guesgen   J. Hertzberg

A Perspective of Constraint-Based Reasoning

An Introductory Tutorial

Springer-Verlag

Berlin Heidelberg New York
London Paris Tokyo
Hong Kong Barcelona
Budapest

Series Editor

Jörg Siekmann
University of Saarland
German Research Center for Artificial Intelligence (DFKI)
Stuhlsatzenhausweg 3, W-6600 Saarbrücken 11, FRG

Volume Editors

Hans Werner Guesgen
Joachim Hertzberg
Gesellschaft für Mathematik und Datenverarbeitung (GMD), Schloß Birlinghoven
Postfach 12 40, W-5205 St. Augustin 1, FRG

CR Subject Classification (1991): I.2.8, I.2.3-4

ISBN 3-540-55510-2 Springer-Verlag Berlin Heidelberg New York
ISBN 0-387-55510-2 Springer-Verlag New York Berlin Heidelberg

© Springer-Verlag Berlin Heidelberg 1992
Printed in Germany

Typesetting: Camera ready by author/editor
Printing and binding: Druckhaus Beltz, Hemsbach/Bergstr.
45/3140-543210 - Printed on acid-free paper

Preface

Constraints are a recurring topic in Artificial Intelligence (AI) about which a wealth of literature has been written. Constraint techniques have been used in many computer programs, and a considerable amount of sub-concepts of constraints, specializations and algorithms have been produced, the relationships between which aren't always as apparent as one would like them to be. So, there seems to be some demand for a more general view of the field.

Our text is an attempt to present many facets of the field in a uniform way. It is based on the material for two tutorials we gave at the 1991 conference of the British Society for the Study of AI and Simulation of Behaviour (AISB91) and at the annual German Workshop on AI in 1991 (GWAI-91).

We would not have been able to write this text outside the creative atmosphere of AI groups like the ones at the German National Research Center for Computer Science (GMD) at Sankt Augustin, Germany, and at the International Computer Science Institute (ICSI) at Berkeley, California, where you have people sitting next-door who are engaged in all these interesting things like nonmonotonic reasoning, connectionism, Boltzmann machines, or reflective systems. In addition, we received fruitful comments and questions from the tutorial participants.

Thanks to Thomas Christaller for allowing us to close our doors for some weeks to write this text. Moreover, we are grateful to our colleagues in the qwertz project on AI planning methods for doing without us for some time: after all, this is not really planning.

The following persons have read preliminary versions of the whole text or of parts of it, resulting in innumerable large and small hints concerning the content, the presentation, or the English style of this text: Ursula Bernhard, Gerd Brewka, Rina Dechter, Jerry Feldman, Manfred Fidelak, Jürgen Kopp, Peter Ladkin, Marc Linster, Christoph Lischka, Gerd Paaß, and Jörg Siekmann.

The work presented in this text is partially funded by the German Federal Ministry for Research and Technology (BMFT) in the joint project TASSO under grant number ITW8900A7. TASSO is also part of the GMD *Leitvorhaben* Assisting Computer (AC).

Sankt Augustin,
March 1992

Hans Werner Guesgen
Joachim Hertzberg

Contents

Chapter 1

Introduction

1.1   What this Text Is About

Much of AI research is about problem solving strategies, for example, developing heuristic search algorithms, reasoning on representations of human knowledge, or performing planning tasks automatically. As a result, several techniques have been crystallized, one of which this text is about: constraint satisfaction or reasoning based on relations.

Constraint-based reasoning is used to solve a widespread field of problems. Some researchers had a certain task in mind and tried to find a method to solve that task efficiently. The Waltz algorithm [Waltz, 1972] is an example from the domain of computer vision. It was intended to interpret polyhedron diagrams as 3D objects in the blocks world. Other domains are, for example,

- circuit analysis [Stallman and Sussman, 1977],

- planning experiments in molecular biology [Stefik, 1981],

- job-shop scheduling [Fox *et al.*, 1982],

- temporal reasoning [Allen, 1983],

- diagnosis [Davis, 1984; Geffner and Pearl, 1987; de Kleer and Williams, 1986],

- and logic programming [Dincbas *et al.*, 1987; Jaffar and Lassez, 1987].

Soon it became clear that constraint satisfaction methods as such are useful and should be provided in form of computer programming languages. An example of such a language is described in G.L. Steele's thesis [1980]. The language is an extension of Lisp by constructs for defining and satisfying constraints. It has many successors, for example, [Gosling, 1983] or [Guesgen, 1989a]. More recently, constraint techniques have been incorporated into logic programming languages, yielding a whole new field of research and application: constraint logic programming [van Hentenryck, 1989].

Not only have the practical aspects of constraint satisfaction been explored in various ways, but also the theoretical ones. The theoretical work has led to results, for example, about the complexity and reducibility of constraint satisfaction problems [Mackworth, 1977; Freuder, 1978] and about the relation between constraint-based reasoning and databases or logic, e.g., [Bibel, 1988; de Kleer, 1989; Guesgen and Ladkin, 1990].

Constraint satisfaction techniques have become part of almost all introductory books on AI, and they can be found in dictionaries, for example, the Encyclopedia of Artificial Intelligence [Shapiro, 1987]. Moreover, whole books have been dedicated to constraint satisfaction; so has been this one. But it is different from others in an important aspect.

Working on practical examples with constraint languages has soon shown that using "mere" constraints is insufficient in several respects. Practical problems tend to yield, for example, inconsistent constraint networks, i.e., the problem is overspecified. In such a case, the constraint language is of little help. Or, as another example, domains may be infinite, rendering constraint approaches inapplicable. There are special adaptations of constraint approaches for these problems, but they are incompatible at first sight. Now, this text is different from others in that it presents all approaches under a common, generalizing view: dynamic constraints.

Actually, dynamic constraints are nothing really new, as we will show that they are no less and no more expressive than the ordinary constraints which you may have heard of already. They are just a new way of viewing constraints as something which has emerged from the attempt to put different constraint approaches under a one roof. However, housing them under this roof also provides new insights about the different approaches separately from each other.

Why did we take the time to write this text? We had the feeling that the possibility of presenting many different areas and approaches of constraint-based reasoning in a uniform way might be interesting in two respects. First, it seems to be a very practical basis for teaching constraint-based reasoning. Second, we think that a uniform view of the constraint world is a good basis for constraint research because it may shed light on aspects or relations of different areas of constraint reasoning that have been neglected so far, thereby simply stimulating new ideas.

One area for such ideas might have to do with the massively parallel implementation of constraint-based reasoning. Certainly this is also feasible with ordinary constraints, but it is the uniformity of dynamic constraint networks, again, that makes following this idea particularly suggestive in our framework. Consequently the chapters on the implementation of constraint-based reasoning contain some hints pointing into this direction.

It must be noted, however, that this text is *not* intended to serve as a self-contained textbook on constraint-based reasoning. It covers most areas of constraint-based reasoning, but in a real textbook, there would have to be, for example, additional parts on applications of constraints, or a more comprehensive treatment on constraint logic programming, which we just sketch as related work (in section 3.4). Moreover, this text does not have the degree of didactic sophistication we would expect from a book serving primarily learning or teaching needs. Let us regard it as a coherent, not really exhaustive text about some interesting view of the field of constraint-based reasoning.

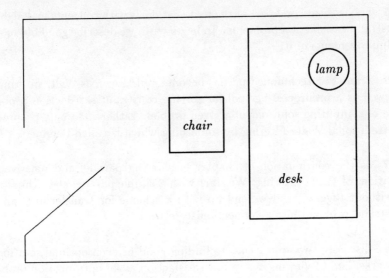

The chair is on the left of the desk on which there is a lamp.

Figure 1.1: Sketch of an office from a bird's-eye view.

1.2   How this Text Is Organized

Chapter 1   which you are reading at the moment is the introduction and also an illustration of our motivation for writing this text. In addition, it shows how the text is organized.

Chapter 2   presents our demo domain for constraint-based reasoning: the office world, or in more precise terms, reasoning about drawings of Spartan office interiors as shown in figure 1.1. Although we use a well-known approach, namely Allen's temporal logic as adapted to spatial relations, the reader should at least a browse through this chapter, since the terminology is slightly changed.

Chapter 3   is the key chapter concerning the notion of dynamic constraints. It defines them and transfers the usual concepts such as solution or consistency to dynamic networks. In addition, it shows their relationship to ordinary constraints.

Chapter 4   is about a special form of constraint manipulation: relaxation which usually deals with inconsistent constraint problems. It is a demonstration of how to represent constraint relaxation in dynamic constraint networks. This concludes the first part of the text, which discusses the relevant notions and presents the material on a more conceptual level.

Chapter 5   starts the second part of the text that deals with concepts and algorithms for *solving* constraint satisfaction problems. To begin with, we describe good old backtracking and some improvements of it.

Chapter 6   refers to a technique that has become well-known as Waltz filtering and that may be viewed as a preprocessing tool for solving constraint satisfaction problems. For the purpose of computing solutions of a given problem rather than only preprocessing it, we extend traditional Waltz filtering by something which is called tagging.

Chapter 7   is the continuation of chapter 6, showing parallel and massively parallel implementations of Waltz filtering. We start with a simple parallel algorithm for filtering with and without tagging, and we end up with a scheme for transforming an arbitrary binary constraint problem into a connectionist network.

Chapter 8   discusses two approaches to finding good or even optimal solutions of constraint networks, i.e., to viewing constraint satisfaction as an optimization problem: simulated annealing and Boltzmann machines. Again, we discuss not only a serial implementation but also a massively parallel one.

Chapter 9   concludes the book with some remarks about spatial reasoning as such—and not just as a demo domain as in this text.

1.3   A Note for the Hasty Reader

Had we thought that our ideas could have been boiled down to 20 pages, we wouldn't have written a book but a 20 pages paper. So, to get all of it, you have to read the whole text.

However, provided that you just want to get an idea of what dynamic constraints are and provided that you are fit in classical constraint approaches, we recommend that you start with the key chapter 3, occasionally referring to the description of our demo domain in chapter 2. After that, you may look at the chapters which are most interesting for you; there are few hard dependencies. We recommend, however, to look at the relaxation chapter 4 before reading the optimization chapter 8 and to consider the chapters 6 and 7, both on filtering approaches with or without tagging, as a unit.

Chapter 2

The Office World

There is no difference between Time and any of the three dimensions of Space except that our consciousness moves along it.

—H.G. Wells: The Time Machine

This chapter pursues two goals. The first and most important is to present the example domain used in different varieties in the text to follow: the office world, consisting of sketches of Spartan office interiors involving windows, desks, chairs, computers, lamps, and the like. Second, we want to give an idea of the area of constraint reasoning informally and *en passant;* the formal and more general introduction to constraints will follow in chapter 3.

We will present the office world as a domain for different basic forms of spatial reasoning. In fact, we will slightly change the problems and the representation from time to time, aiming at simple and intuitive problems to be dealt with in the respective chapters. So, there isn't *the* office world. (But that seems to be frequent: There isn't *the* blocks world either.) Note that we do *not* intend to follow all the intricacies of spatial reasoning in general, nor even address them all. This is a text about constraints, not spatial reasoning! We just found the office world to be as intuitive as the blocks world, yet more interesting in itself and a little bit closer to reality. Experts in spatial reasoning may argue that our office world *is* some blocks world; this is true, but it serves our needs which are, in this setting, more of a didactic nature with respect to constraint reasoning.

2.1 Types of Spatial Reasoning

A precise, spatial description of an office, for example, may be obtained by describing the shapes and the positions of the objects in the office by three-dimensional equations. This of course may be very complex and is not a cognitively plausible description of the domain (whatever "cognitively plausible" is in detail). A human being would describe an office in a more qualitative way: the pencils are in the upper right drawer of the desk which is in front of the window; on the left of it you will find a bookcase containing manuals; and so on. You might, for example, describe the rough sketch of an office as given in figure 2.1

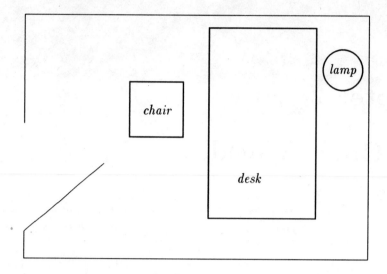

Figure 2.1: A sketch of an office from a bird's-eye view.

by the following proposition:

The chair is left of both the desk and the lamp, and the desk is left of the lamp.

Based on such a proposition, you could do the following form of reasoning, which might be termed spatial. For the sake of simplicity, we restrict ourselves not only to a one-dimensional space but also to the case that the objects are viewed as points rather than as items occupying physical space.

Assume that it is the task to find a position to place each of the objects chair, desk, and lamp, where there is only a finite set of possible positions. The *left of* relations between the objects *chair*, *desk*, and *lamp* can then be said to *constrain* the positions of the objects. So, these relationships can be represented by a constraint network on the variables *chair*, *desk*, and *lamp*, where each variable specifies the distance of the respective object to a reference point on some horizontal axis. The constraints between the variables are the restrictions according to the above relationships, i.e., the constraint between *chair* and *desk*, for example, allows only those tuples (d_{chair}, d_{desk}) of domain elements of the variables *chair* and *desk* for which $d_{chair} < d_{desk}$ holds. Figure 2.2 shows a graph of the constraint network, the circles representing the variables and the rectangles representing the constraints. Suppose that the domains

$$D_{chair} = \{4, 5, 6\} \qquad D_{desk} = \{5, 6, 7\} \qquad D_{lamp} = \{6, 7, 8\}$$

are associated with the variables *chair*, *desk*, and *lamp*, respectively. Then, the assignments *chair* = 4, *desk* = 7, and *lamp* = 8 are a solution of the constraint network, i.e., $(4, 7, 8)$ represents admissible positions of *chair*, *desk*, and *lamp*.

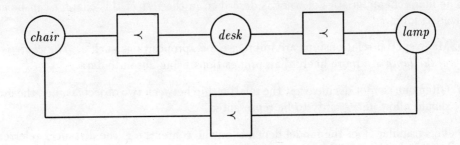

Figure 2.2: Constraint network representing spatial relationships.

You can see a few more intricate features of the constraint network in figure 2.2. For example, for every value of every variable, you can find other values for another variable such that the constraint between these two variables is satisfied; e.g., for *chair* = 5, you can choose *lamp* = 7. This property is called 2-consistency for the number of variables involved. The exact definition of 2-consistency will be presented in chapter 3.

However, the network is not 3-consistent, as we will see, since not every pair of consistent values can be extended to a consistent triple. For example, the assignment *chair* = 6 and *lamp* = 7, which is consistent with respect to the constraint between *chair* and *lamp*, makes it impossible to select a value for *desk* such that all constraints are satisfied. The same holds for *chair* = 5 and *lamp* = 6: this combination cannot be extended to a solution either.

On the other hand, there are no values in D_{chair}, D_{desk}, and D_{lamp} that can be deleted without reducing the set of solutions. Thus, it is impossible to obtain an equivalent 3-consistent network, i.e., a 3-consistent network with the same set of solutions, by restricting variable domains. The remedy, of course, is to tighten the $\prec$ constraint between *chair* and *lamp* such that tuples like (5, 6) and (6, 7) are no longer admissible. All this is the sort of reasoning you can do with constraints, and we will present the basis for it in the text to follow.

Besides reasoning about positions of objects, there is another useful form of spatial reasoning: reasoning about relationships between objects like

The chair is left of both the desk and the lamp, and the desk is left of the lamp.

This form of reasoning might be closer to what the intuitive meaning of the term spatial reasoning is.

It is obvious that such propositions do not describe a given scenario as precisely and completely as quantitative mathematical formulas do. In many contexts, such abstract, qualitative descriptions are a useful means of describing, for example, physical relationships in a way easy to manipulate (cf., e.g., the work in qualitative physics [Weld and de Kleer, 1990]). Beyond that, it seems that commonsense reasoning often is of a qualitative nature rather than a quantitative one.

The main characteristics of what is described in the rest of this chapter can be summarized as follows:[1]

- Many spatial relationships are imprecise, i.e., propositions such as *The chair is left of the lamp* are more likely than propositions using absolute data.

- Often one cannot decide what the relationship between two objects is, i.e., the model should allow uncertainty to be represented.

- The granularity of the model depends on the context, e.g. the distances referred to in *The chair is left of the lamp* and in *The t key is left of the y key on the computer keyboard* are certainly different.

The key idea is to specify spatial relationships between objects (as opposed to determining the spatial position of an object absolutely), each relationship split into several components. Consider, for example, the office to be described by two-component relationships. One component may specify the left-right relation between two objects, the other component may be used to distiguish between front and rear. The relation between a bookcase and a window can then, for example, be described by the pair ⟨*left of, in front of*⟩ if the bookcase is left of and in front of the window.

We will not address the problem of choosing an adequate reference frame (or orientation frame as it is called in [Kuipers, 1977]) here. A reference frame determines the direction in which two objects are related to each other. For instance, the left-right and front-rear axes in the above examples specify such a reference frame. In [Retz-Schmidt, 1988], several kinds of reference frames are discussed: intrinsic, extrinsic, and deictic ones. An intrinsic reference frame uses one of the objects to determine the direction of the relation. For example, the intrinsic interpretation of *The desk is in front of the chair* results in a relational description that depends on the direction in which the chair is pointing. If an extrinsic reference frame is used, the relational description is expressed with respect to, for example, the orientation of the person sitting on the chair or the direction in which the chair is moving. If not stated otherwise, we will use deictic reference frames in the following, i.e., the relational descriptions are those observed from some external viewpoint.

In the next section, we will introduce the basic, one-dimensional spatial relations, followed by a description of the constraint-based reasoning mechanisms which may be applied to them. Then, we will show how higher order relations are constructed and how these relations may be obtained from scenarios.

2.2   The Basic Spatial Relations

Allen [1983] defined a set of temporal relations to describe interrelationships between time intervals such as *Interval I_1 is before interval I_2*. Since there is a direct isomorphism between physical structures of time and one-dimensional spatial structures, the definition of one-dimensional spatial relations is straightforward. Figure 2.3 shows the set of relations

---

[1]The characteristics are similar to those listed in [Allen, 1983]. Although Allen discussed aspects of temporal reasoning rather than spatial reasoning, one can view his approach as the one-dimensional analog to the three-dimensional descriptions used here.

Relationship	Symbol	Symbol for Converse	Picture
O_1 *left of* O_2	$\prec$	$\succ$	
O_1 *attached to* O_2	$\preceq$	$\succeq$	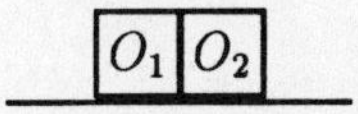
O_1 *overlapping* O_2	$\Leftarrow$	$\Rightarrow$	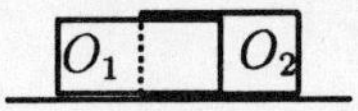
O_1 *inside* O_2	$\sqsubset$	$\sqsupset$	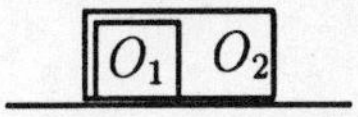

Figure 2.3: The possible relationships between two objects.

we want to use here.[2] It is obvious that any spatial relationship between two objects can be represented by this set and—since the relations are disjoint—the representation is unique.

The eight relations described in figure 2.3 do not suffice to describe spatial interrelationships in every case, i.e., a larger set of relations may be necessary. Consider, for example, the propositions *The chair is very, very, very far away from the desk* and *The chair is close to the desk but does not touch it*. They both have the same representation in our model, namely:

$$(chair \prec desk) \vee (chair \succ desk)$$

We will use the usual shorthand notation in the sequel, abbreviating a disjunction of relations by a set of relations, for example:

$$chair \quad \{\prec, \succ\} \quad desk$$

If the propositions were to be distinguished, the model would have to be extended. Nevertheless, we will restrict ourselves to the eight relations here so that the examples are easy to read.

A set of spatial propositions can be represented as a network consisting—as before—of two different types of nodes: circles representing the objects and rectangles representing the relations (the network in figure 2.4 shows some examples). Reasoning about spatial relationships in a constraint reasoning setting now can be viewed as modifying the labels of the rectangles, i.e., the constraints, and inserting new constraints into the network. Consider, for example, the network of figure 2.5(A), which is an extension of the one in figure 2.4. Since O_4 is between O_1 and O_3, intuitively the spatial relation between O_1

---

[2]The relation *left of* is equivalent to Allen's *before*. Its meaning depends on the dimension which is considered and may be one of *left of*, *below*, or *in front of*. Note that none of the relations is symmetrical, although this might be suggested by names like *attached to* or *overlapping*: the proposition O_1 *is attached to* O_2 should read O_1 *is attached to* O_2 *such that* O_1 *is left*; the same holds for *overlapping*.

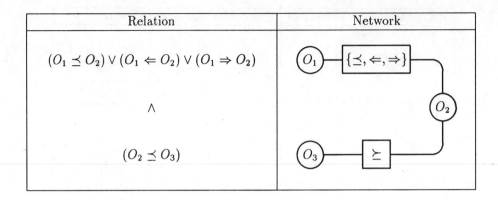

Figure 2.4: Representation of spatial relationships in a constraint network.

and O_3 must be $O_1 \prec O_3$ (cf. figure 2.5(B)). From this, together with $O_2 \preceq O_3$, we can conclude that $\Rightarrow$ is not a possible relation between O_1 and O_2, because O_1 is at least as far left as O_2 (cf. figure 2.5(C)).

The example shows that there are two different reasoning steps on a network of spatial relations:

1. Computing the composition of spatial relations, i.e., inserting new constraints into the network. A result of such a step would be, for example, the $\prec$ constraint between O_1 and O_3 shown in figure 2.5(B).

2. Deleting all relations that are inconsistent. In figure 2.5(C), $\Rightarrow$ has been deleted from the constraint between O_1 and O_2, since it is incompatible with the $\prec$ constraint between O_1 and O_3 and the $\succeq$ constraint between O_3 and O_2.

The first step can be subsumed by the second one in the following way: instead of the original network we consider the corresponding complete network. A complete network is one with constraints between each pair of variables. It is obvious that such a network can be easily obtained by inserting rectangles labeled with the set of all spatial relations.

The composition table shown in figure 2.6 defines constraints that must hold in a network of spatial relations. It is similar to the transitivity table in [Allen, 1983].[3] The entries in the table describe the possible relations between O_1 and O_3 depending on the relations between O_1 and O_2 as well as O_2 and O_3. A question mark means that the relation between O_1 and O_3 may be any of the eight possible relations.

Standard constraint satisfaction algorithms can be used to remove inconsistencies from the network. These algorithms result in different levels of consistency (ranging from local consistency to global consistency, cf. [Mackworth, 1977]), and they are of different complexity (up to exponential). Allen [1983] has introduced an algorithm that guarantees

---

[3]In [Allen, 1983], the term *transitivity table* is used instead of *composition table*. However, we prefer to use *composition table* since it is in accordance with the notion of composition in [Montanari, 1974] and since the term *transitivity table* may be confused with the property of a relation being transitive.

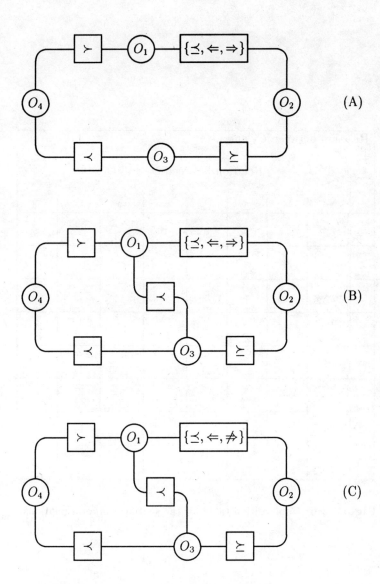

Figure 2.5: Reasoning about spatial relationships.

Relation between O_1 and O_2
↓

Relation between O_2 and O_3

	≺	≻	≼	≽	⇐	⇒	⊏	⊐
≺	≺	?	≺	≺,≼ ⇐,⊏	≺	≺,≼ ⇐,⊏	≺,≼ ⇐,⊏	≺
≻	?	≻	≻,≽ ⇒,⊏	≻	≻,≽ ⇒,⊏	≻	≻,≽ ⇒,⊏	≻
≼	≺	≻,≽ ⇒,⊐	≺	⊏ ⊐	≺	⊏ ⇐	≼,⇐ ⊏	≺ ≼
≽	≺,≼ ⇐,⊐	≻	⊏ ⊐	≻	⇒ ⊏	≻	≽,⇒ ⊏	≻ ≽
⇐	≺	≻,≽ ⇒,⊐	≺	⇒ ⊐	≺,≼ ⇐	⇐,⇒ ⊏,⊐	⇐ ⊏	≺,≼ ⇐,⊐
⇒	≺,≼ ⇐,⊐	≻	⇐ ⊐	≻	⇐,⇒ ⊏,⊐	≻,≽ ⇒	⇒ ⊏	≻,≽ ⇒,⊐
⊏	≺	≻	≺ ≼	≻ ≽	≺,≼ ⇐,⊏	≻,≽ ⇒,⊏	⊏	?
⊐	≺,≼ ⇐,⊐	≻,≽ ⇒,⊐	≼,⇐ ⊐	≽,⇒ ⊐	⇐ ⊐	⇒ ⊐	⇐,⇒ ⊏,⊐	⊐

Figure 2.6: Composition table for the spatial/temporal relations.

consistency in all three node subnetworks of the entire network and that takes $O(n^3)$ time. All this will be explained below.

So far, we have sketched how to specify spatial relationships and how to perform spatial reasoning. However, our models are still restricted in that they are suitable only for one-dimensional relationships. In the following, we will extend them to two-dimensional and three-dimensional models, showing how the algorithms can be applied to such models with only some more effort.

2.3   Higher-Dimensional Models

There is a straightforward extension of one-dimensional models to models regarding two or three dimensions: each spatial relation is replaced with a tuple (pair or triple) of spatial relations, each component describing an aspect of the multi-dimensional, spatial relationship. For example, consider again figure 1.1, showing the sketch of an office with a desk, a chair, and a lamp.

Let us assume that a two-dimensional representation of the spatial relationships between pairs of objects is to be obtained. The canonical way to get such a representation is to introduce two orthogonal axes (a horizontal x-axis and a vertical y-axis) and to describe the spatial relations with respect to the x-axis and the y-axis, respectively. This may result in the following spatial descriptions:

$$chair \quad \langle \prec, \sqsubset \rangle \quad desk$$
$$desk \quad \langle \sqsupset, \sqsupset \rangle \quad lamp$$

We can now apply the composition table to the components of the relation pairs, which yields an additional spatial description:

$$chair \quad \langle \prec, ? \rangle \quad lamp$$

To remove the ambiguity in the relation between *chair* and *lamp*, one must extract additional information from the sketch.

The spatial descriptions can be checked for consistency, applying constraint satisfaction methods to the components of the relation tuples. This is of the same complexity as in the one-dimensional case, since the components are considered independently. The disadvantage of this method is that certain ambiguities cannot be expressed tightly enough. Consider, for example, the proposition shown in figure 2.7. A model of the spatial relationships expressed by the proposition is given by:

$$lamp \quad \langle \{\sqsubset, \prec\}, \{\sqsubset, \succ\} \rangle \quad desk$$

It is obvious that this model allows other interpretations as well, e.g. the one shown in figure 2.8.

A way to solve the problem of ambiguity is to use sets of tuples of spatial relations rather than tuples of sets, e.g. instead of the above term we could use

$$lamp \quad \{\langle \sqsubset, \sqsubset \rangle, \langle \prec, \succ \rangle\} \quad desk$$

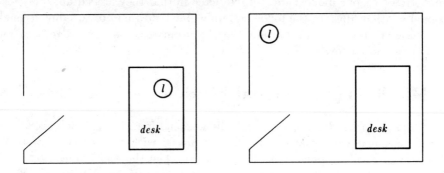

The lamp is either on the desk or in the corner opposite the desk.

Figure 2.7: Sketches of an office with two alternative locations for the lamp.

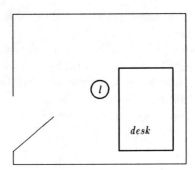

Figure 2.8: Another place where the lamp might be.

Even without having actually seen an algorithm for constraint satisfaction, you may suspect that this leads to a quadratic deterioration of the algorithms[4] and can result in combinatorial explosion which we want to avoid. However, we can try to apply the sets-of-tuples algorithms, hoping that combinatorial explosion does not occur, or we can use the tuples-of-sets algorithms as a preprocessing method.

2.4 Some Other Work

There is some work that is directly related to what we have described in this chapter. The approach closest to our work is the one in [Freksa, 1990], where the same set of relations is used as in [Allen, 1983]. Freksa could show that not all combinations of spatial relations are plausible, since some of them do not occur in the real world. By restricting himself to konvex sets of relations ($\{\prec, \preceq, \Leftarrow\}$, for example, is a konvex set but $\{\prec, \succ\}$ is not), he could restrict the complexity of the constraint satisfaction algorithms significantly.

In [1990], Hernández introduced an extension of Allen's approach to represent the spatial features occurring in 2D projections of 3D scenes. He suggested to establish spatial relations between objects by splitting them up into two aspects: projection and orientation. The aspect of projection describes the distance between the objects in a way similar to the one introduced in this chapter. The aspect of orientation states how the objects are located to each other.

The work described in [Mukerjee and Joe, 1990] is very similar to Hernández' approach. There, objects of a two-dimensional world are characterized by the directions into which the objects are moving and by associating trajectories with the objects along which they are moving (the authors call them *lines of support* or *lines of travel*). The direction of an object defines orthogonal coordinate axes which divide the plane into four quadrants with the object in its center. Two objects can be related to each other with respect to their directions as follows: Take the quadrants of one object and determine into which quadrant the direction of the other object is pointing.

Beyond that, the trajectories of two objects are compared with each other if they define a so-called collision parallelogram (cf. figure 2.9). The position of the collision parallelogram with respect to either of the objects can be described by a one-dimensional relation from the set of Allen's relations.[5] Since in general the position of the collision parallelogram with respect to object O_1 is different to the one with respect to object O_2, both of them must be considered.

Maddux [1989] defined algebras on points in the Euclidean space $I\!R^n$, called compass algebras. In the two-dimensional case, for example, a certain compass algebra contains all those relations that are obtained by applying union, intersection, complementation, composition, and converse to the relations *east* and *north*, where *east* and *north* are defined as follows:

$$
\begin{aligned}
east &= \{(\langle x, y \rangle, \langle x', y \rangle) \mid x, x', y \in I\!R \wedge x < x'\} \\
north &= \{(\langle x, y \rangle, \langle x, y' \rangle) \mid x, y, y' \in I\!R \wedge y < y'\}
\end{aligned}
$$

---

[4]Instead of $2 * C_A(n)$, we obtain $C_A(n)^2$, where $C_A(n)$ is the complexity of an algorithm A in the one-dimensional case applied to a network with n nodes.

[5]In fact, Mukerjee and Joe use a set of relations that is slightly different to the one used in [Allen, 1983]. This enables them to reduce the complexity of their reasoning algorithm.

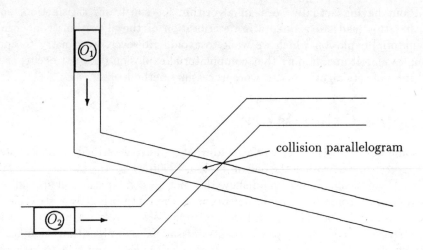

Figure 2.9: Two objects and their spatial trajectories (from [Mukerjee and Joe, 1990]).

He shows that constraint satisfaction in any compass algebra is NP-complete for two or more dimensions.

In [Malik and Binford, 1983], spatial interrelationships are specified by linear constraints, i.e., linear inequalities between boundary surfaces of objects. Spatial reasoning is then based on linear programming applying the simplex algorithm. A technique similar to ours is used to derive three-dimensional descriptions from one-dimensional ones.

Egenhofer [1991] describes the relationship between two objects by relating certain aspects (interior, boundary, and closure) of one object to aspects of the other object, yielding 3×3 matrices in which each entry denotes whether the intersection of the corresponding aspects is empty or not. When certain restrictions are applied (e.g., there are no holes in the objects), only 8 different matrices occur, each corresponding to a Allen relation.

Spatial reasoning as presented here is based on Allen's [1983] work on relational *temporal* reasoning. This is a link to a whole bunch of related work: temporal reasoning with constraints. A more recent paper on that issue containing further references is [Dechter *et al.*, 1991]. Additional references and more general aspects of temporal and spatial reasoning can be found in chapter 9.

Chapter 3

Constraint Concepts

This chapter introduces the basic notions of constraint reasoning like, e.g., constraint, constraint network, solution, and consistency. We will use a non-standard formulation, namely, *dynamic constraints*. We will show that this formulation is equivalent, from a theoretical point of view, to the ordinary formulation, and we will show how to map the different formulations to each other. Thus, this chapter also introduces the ordinary view on constraints, in a way.

However, if our formulation is theoretically not more expressive than the ordinary one, why use it? The reason is *practical* expressivity. As we have sketched in the previous chapter, the ordinary view on constraints makes a difference between variables and constraints (or *relations* on these variables). In dynamic constraints, there is no such difference, and we will see that this makes it very easy to understand constraint satisfaction, constraint manipulation, and constraint relaxation, which are usually considered to be different things, as essentially the *same* thing.

Since dynamic constraints can be defined as simply as ordinary ones, we think the only reason for *not* using them is not being familiar with them. This is what we want to remedy in this chapter. However, as it is ordinary constraints that are mostly used in the constraint literature and as they can be considered to be an important special case of dynamic constraints to which we will come back frequently, we start our definition of the basic notions of constraint reasoning with defining *them*.

3.1   Constraints and Networks

In section 2.1, we have sketched that an (ordinary) constraint is just a relation on a set of variables. This is indeed the definition of an ordinary constraint:

Def. 1 (Ordinary Constraint)
A k-ary (ordinary) constraint C is a pair consisting of a k-elementary set of variables $\{V_1, \ldots, V_k\}$ over domains $D_1, \ldots, D_k$ and a decidable relation $R \subseteq D_1 \times \cdots \times D_k$.

Instead of ordinary constraints, we will sometimes speak of *classical* constraints. An example is the $\prec$ constraint between the variables *chair* and *desk* in section 2.1.

As we have seen, e.g., in figure 2.2, constraints are connected to constraint networks by sharing variables, which is easily expressed in the following definition.

Def. 2 (Ordinary Constraint Network)
An (ordinary) constraint network is a pair consisting of a set of variables $\{V_1, \ldots, V_m\}$ and a set of ordinary constraints $\{C_1, \ldots, C_n\}$, the variables of each C_i being a subset of $\{V_1, \ldots, V_m\}$.

Let us now define dynamic constraints and dynamic constraint networks. The key idea is to build networks of nodes of a uniform type: dynamic constraints. The intuition behind these nodes is that they represent relations which are characterized by enumerating relation elements. Both variables and constraints of ordinary constraint networks are subsumed by dynamic constraints. What has been the domain of a variable in an ordinary constraint now becomes the extension of a relation (dynamic constraints are defined by specifying the extension of their relation, too). The relation of an ordinary constraint becomes the relation of a dynamic one, and what has been the link between a constraint and a variable before, now becomes a dependency of dynamic constraints on other ones.

The definition of dynamic constraints, hence, is analogous to the definition of ordinary ones. A little difference: since dynamic constraints are to be used both as constraints and variables, their arity is not restricted to a positive integer but may also be zero:[1]

Def. 3 (Dynamic Constraint)
A k-ary dynamic constraint C is a pair consisting of a set of dynamic constraints $\delta(C)$, and a decidable relation $R \subseteq D$ for some domain D. $\delta(C)$ is called the set of dependents of C, R is called C's constraint relation, and D is C's domain. $\delta(C)$, R, and D are restricted as follows:

- *If $k = 0$, then $\delta(C) = \emptyset$, and R is arbitrary.*

- *If $k > 0$, then $\delta(C) = \{C_1, \ldots, C_k\}$, and $D = D_1 \times \cdots \times D_k$, where D_i is the domain of C_i.*

We say that a dynamic constraint is connected with its dependents, if any, by *dependency* links. Note that a constraint C cannot depend on itself, neither directly nor indirectly, since the relations of C's dependents are projections to the components of C's relation. A graphical representation of a dynamic constraint with its dependents is given in figure 3.1.

You might ask what the *dynamic* aspect of dynamic constraints is. The answer is that there is usually some sort of "downward flow" of information in ordinary constraints (particularly in filtering, see chapter 6): the ordinary constraints determine admissible values for their variables. In dynamic constraint networks, the information flow is more

---

[1]In the definition, it would be more accurate to say: *consisting of a set $\delta(C)$ of dependencies to dynamic constraints* instead of *consisting of a set of dynamic constraints $\delta(C)$*, which might cause problems with infinite chains of different dependents. However, we prefer the latter, since it is more readable and in analogy to ordinary constraints, and we will restrict ourselves to considering finite sets of dynamic constraints later on.

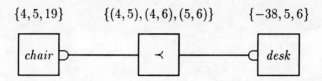

$$\{4, 5, 19\} \qquad \{(4,5),(4,6),(5,6)\} \qquad \{-38, 5, 6\}$$

Figure 3.1: A dynamic constraint called $\prec$ with its dependent 0-ary dynamic constraints, where all relations are annotated. Here and in all following figures, a constraint C is a dependent of constraint C' if the edge between C and C' is marked with a $\supset$ at the end joining C.

symmetric because all elements, i.e., all dynamic constraints are conceptually equal, and it is very natural to let the dependents determine the relation of the dynamic constraint they depend on. Note that this is mostly a difference in emphasis, not in principle.

In an ordinary constraint network, the constraints are connected via variables. Since dynamic constraints take the place of both variables and constraints, they must be connected directly, which is of course realized by the dependency relation.

Def. 4 (Dynamic Constraint Network)
A dynamic constraint network is a finite set of dynamic constraints $C_1, \ldots, C_n$ that is closed under dependency, i.e.: $\forall i \in \{1, \ldots, n\} : \delta(C_i) \subseteq \{C_1, \ldots, C_n\}$

Figure 3.2 shows a dynamic constraint network for the office scenario of figure 2.1.

Now, the interesting question is: how do dynamic constraints relate to ordinary constraints and how about the power of dynamic networks compared with the power of ordinary networks? The answer is: the two versions of constraints are equally expressive from a theoretical point of view. We will show that by explaining how to transform ordinary into dynamic networks, and vice versa.

To start with, each ordinary constraint network can be represented by a dynamic network in the following way:

1. Each variable of the given constraint network is mapped to a 0-ary dynamic constraint with the variable's domain as relation.

2. Each constraint of the given network is mapped to a dynamic constraint of the same arity and with the same relation. The dependents of the dynamic constraint are the dynamic constraints that are the translations of the variables of the given constraint.

We therefore define:

Def. 5 (Translated Dynamic Constraint Network)
Let N be an ordinary constraint network and N' be a dynamic network. Then N' is called a translation of N, if

- *N' contains a 0-ary dynamic constraint for each variable of N with the variable's domain as relation,*

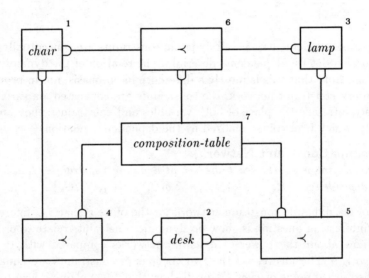

Figure 3.2: Dynamic constraint network for the office scenario. Relations of the dynamic constraints *chair*, *desk*, and *lamp* are unary integer relations such as $\{4, 5, 6\}$; relations of the $\prec$ dynamic constraints could be *less than* relations on integers such as $\{(4, 5), (5, 6), (4, 6)\}$; and the relation of the *composition-table* constraint could be the composition table such as in figure 2.6.

- N' contains a dynamic constraint C' for each constraint C of N, the arity and the relation of C' being equal to the arity of C and the dependents of C' being the translations of the variables of C, and

- N' contains no further dynamic constraints.

We will call translated dynamic constraint networks *translated networks* for short.

Dynamic constraint networks can be extended easily to include additional constraints. For example, the network shown in figure 3.2 is a translation of the ordinary network shown in figure 2.2, extended by a constraint that represents Allen's composition table.

Let us now turn to the question whether every dynamic network has an ordinary counterpart. This question may seem less simple because dynamic networks may come in arbitrarily many layers of dependency, whereas ordinary constraints just have the two layers of variables and (ordinary) constraints. However, the multi-layer structure of dynamic networks can be boiled down to the two layer ordinary network structure. To show this, we introduce the notions of a *corresponding constraint* and a *corresponding constraint network*. The idea is to view relation elements of higher order dynamic constraints as variable values in ordinary networks and to introduce this variable, which just has a more complex domain, as an additional place into all relations. This reflects the fact that not only the relations of a dynamic constraint and its dependents but also the way in which they are connected is captured in a corresponding ordinary constraint.

Def. 6 (Corresponding Ordinary Constraint)
Let C be a dynamic constraint with dependents $C_1, \ldots, C_k$ over domains $D_1, \ldots, D_k$, respectively, and let $R \subseteq D_1 \times \cdots \times D_k$ be the relation of C. An ordinary constraint C' on $k+1$ variables with relation $R' \subseteq D_1 \times \cdots \times D_k \times (D_1 \times \cdots \times D_k)$ is called a corresponding constraint of C, if it is defined as follows:

- *if $k > 0$, then $R' = \{(d_1, \ldots, d_k, (d_1, \ldots, d_k)) \mid (d_1, \ldots, d_k) \in R\}$*

- *if $k = 0$, then $R' = R$*

The term *corresponding ordinary constraint* will be abbreviated as *corresponding constraint*.

With this definition of a corresponding constraint in mind, the definition of a corresponding network is straightforward:

Def. 7 (Corresponding Constraint Network)
Let $N = \{C_1, \ldots, C_n\}$ be a dynamic constraint network, where D_i is the domain of C_i. Let N' be an ordinary constraint network over variables $V_1, \ldots, V_n$. N' is a corresponding constraint network of N, if

- *the domain of V_i is D_i,*

- *for every dynamic constraint $C_i \in N$, N' contains a corresponding constraint C'_i, and*

- *N' contains no further constraints.*

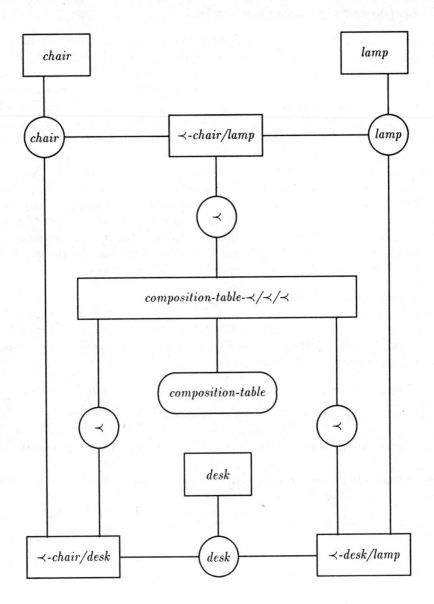

Figure 3.3: A corresponding network of the office scenario constraint network in figure 3.2.

Obviously, for each dynamic constraint network, there is a corresponding ordinary constraint network. The recipe how to build it is given by definition 7. However, the corresponding network may look a little bit clumsy. Reconsider, for example, the network of figure 3.2, a corresponding network of which is shown in figure 3.3. The dynamic constraints of the original network have been replaced with variables. In addition, equally many new constraints have been inserted that encode the dependency structure as well as the relations of the original dynamic network. The $\prec$-*chair/desk* constraint, for example, states that the relation between the variables *chair* and *desk* is equal to $\prec$.

So we have seen that ordinary and dynamic constraint networks can be transformed into each other. In the following, we will define all relevant concepts for dynamic constraints, not ordinary ones; most of these notions are also defined for ordinary constraints and can be applied to them by considering ordinary constraints as special cases of dynamic ones. (We will, however, talk about the important special case of ordinary constraints from time to time.)

3.2 Solutions and their Generating Sets

A solution is what you, in most cases, expect a constraint network to deliver. For an ordinary network, a solution intuitively is a tuple of values such that every variable is assigned one value and all (ordinary) constraints are satisfied for this value combination. The intuition is the same for dynamic networks, but we must use a more symmetrical definition of the notion of solution here: a solution of a dynamic constraint network is a tuple that

1. consists of components that are elements of the domains of the respective dynamic constraints and

2. satisfies all dynamic constraints in the network.

Formally, this is captured in the following definition, where we start with the second point, defining satisfaction. Note that π_l denotes the projection on the lth component of a tuple.

Def. 8 (Satisfaction, Solution)
Given a set of dynamic constraints $M = \{C_1, \ldots, C_m\}$ over domains $D_1, \ldots, D_m$ with relations $R_1 \subseteq D_1, \ldots, R_m \subseteq D_m$, then a tuple $(d_1, \ldots, d_m) \in R_1 \times \cdots \times R_m$ satisfies $C_i \in M$ if

- *all dependents of C_i are in M*

- *if C_j is the lth dependent of C_i, then $\pi_l(d_i) = d_j$*

The tuple $(d_1, \ldots, d_m)$ is called a solution of M if it satisfies all constraints in M.

The task of finding one, some, or every solution of a dynamic constraint network is called a *dynamic constraint satisfaction problem* (dynCSP); we sometimes use the terms dynamic constraint network and dynCSP interchangeably if this causes no confusion. The analog to dynCSPs in the case of ordinary networks is called (ordinary) constraint satisfaction problem (CSP). A dynCSP should not be confused with a dynamic constraint satisfaction problem (DCSP) as used, for example, in [Dechter and Dechter, 1988] and [Bessière, 1991]. A DCSP is a sequence of *static*, i.e., ordinary CSPs, where a CSP in the sequence results from the preceeding one by adding or deleting constraints.

In general, the solution of a dynamic constraint network has more constituents than the solution of an ordinary constraint network (which is usually defined to be a tuple of values for all variables) since all nodes of the network participate in it rather than only the subclass of nodes that are variables. For example, a solution for the network of figure 2.2—assuming appropriate variable coverings—is $(4, 5, 6)$, whereas—assuming the order indicated by the superscripts in figure 3.2—the corresponding solution for the dynamic network is:

$$(4, \; 5, \; 6, \; (4,5), \; (5,6), \; (4,6), \; ((4,5), \; (5,6), \; (4,6))) \tag{3.1}$$

Moreover—assuming the appropriate order of the variables—, this is also a solution for the corresponding network in figure 3.3.

One may argue that we have cheated a little here. The composition table constraint was defined in terms of the basic spatial relations like $\prec$ or $\Rightarrow$, not pairs of integers. By selling (3.1) as a solution for the network in figure 3.2, we tacitly assume that the basic spatial relations can and must also be defined extensionally, i.e., by enumerating their elements. This is certainly possible, but very clumsy for realistic applications. In such applications, there is no way around defining the spatial relations *intensionally* and to take care of the link between the intensional relation definition in the composition table constraint and elements of their extensions to be dealt with in its dependent spatial relation constraints.

A generalization of this idea is the following. The extensions of spatial relations may be viewed as quantitative information, whereas Allen's descriptions are of qualitative nature. The goal then is to combine quantitative and qualitative information in one constraint network. Of course, using the extensions of spatial relations is not the only way to incorporate quantitative information about spatial relations into the constraint network. Another possibility is to describe distances between objects in form of inequalities and to combine these with qualitative information à la Allen. This idea has been elaborated in the area of temporal reasoning, for example, in [Kautz and Ladkin, 1991] and [Meiri, 1991].

The problem of intensional versus extensional descriptions is not just a problem of spatial reasoning but a more general problem whenever you build hierarchies of relations: The extensions of the relations grow the larger the higher you go, and the desire of describing them intensionally may get stronger. However, most concepts and algorithms presented here assume that, e.g., dependent dynamic constraints in a dynamic network be described extensionally; in other words, only the topmost dynamic constraints in the dependency hierarchy may be described intensionally. We cannot solve this problem here, only address it. But note that it is no problem of *dynamic* constraints in particular: You can find it in ordinary constraints, too. The hierarchy in the network is just flatter there—namely, two levels—so that the problem may be a bit softer.

Obviously, writing down the solution of a dynamic network as in (3.1) is heavily redundant, essentially consisting in assigning 4, 5, and 6 to the respective 0-ary dynamic constraints and "setting the rest appropriately". This is, in fact, what is usually done in ordinary constraints by defining a solution to consist of just variable assignments and to leave implicit which relation elements in the ordinary constraints of the ordinary constraint network are triggered by these assignments. In short: the same is true for dynamic networks. It is sufficient to specify just a *subset* of the components to determine the whole solution uniquely. For example, the above solution can be constructed when the first three components, namely 4, 5, and 6, are given. The constraints that belong to these components are a generating set from which the values of the remaining constraints can be computed by combination and projection. This idea is captured in the following definition:

Def. 9 (Generating Set, Resulting Set)

Given a dynamic constraint network N and sets of dynamic constraints $N_g, N_r \subseteq N$, then N_g is called a generating set of N_r, if every solution of N_r can be reconstructed by combination of and projection onto components of a solution of N_g.

N_r is called the resulting set of N_g with respect to N (for short: $\rho_N(N_g)$), if N_g is a generating set of N_r, and no superset of N_r in N is generated by N_g.

For example, $\{chair, desk, lamp\}$ is a generating set for the network shown in figure 3.2, and so are:

- the $\prec$ constraints between *chair* and *desk* and between *desk* and *lamp*,

- *chair* and the $\prec$ constraint between *desk* and *lamp*, or

- the composition table constraint.

In general, the set $\{C_1, \ldots, C_n\}$ of all constraints of a given network is a generating set (though not a minimal one), and so is the subset of $\{C_1, \ldots, C_n\}$ that contains the 0-ary dynamic constraints, i.e., all constraints without dependents (or the set of variables in the ordinary case):

Prop. 1 (Special Generating Sets)

Given a network N of dynamic constraints, let M be the subset of all 0-ary constraints, i.e., $M = \{C \mid C \in N \wedge \delta(C) = \emptyset\}$. Then both N and M are generating sets.

Proof: N is a generating set by definition. That M is a generating set follows from definition 8: the relation of each constraint with arity greater than zero is composed (directly or indirectly) of relation elements of 0-ary dynamic constraints.
□

Two other rather obvious "linearity" properties of generating sets and resulting sets are captured in the following propositions:

Prop. 2 (Subsets of Resulting Sets)

Given a dynamic constraint network N and sets of dynamic constraints $N_g, N_r \subseteq N$. If N_r is a resulting set of N_g w.r.t. N, then the resulting set of a subset of N_g w.r.t. N is a subset of N_r.

Proof: Let N'_g be a subset of N_g and N'_r be the resulting set of N'_g. N'_r is generated by N'_g and each superset of N'_g, thus also by N_g. Since N_r is the set of all constraints that can be generated from N_g, N'_r must be a subset of N_r.
$\square$

Prop. 3 (Supersets of Generating Sets)
Let N_g be a generating set of N, and let N' be a superset of N. Then N_g can be extended to a generating set of N' by adding at most constraints from $N' \setminus N$.

Proof: Let $N'_g = N_g \cup N' \setminus N$, then N'_g is an extension of N_g by constraints from $N' \setminus N$ and also a generating set of N'.
$\square$

With the definitions of a generating set/resulting set and the above propositions, we can now define the notion of solution equivalence of ordinary and dynamic networks and prove it for pairs of ordinary/translated and dynamic/corresponding networks. The idea of solution equivalence is that each solution of the ordinary network uniquely determines a solution of the dynamic network and vice versa:

Def. 10 (Solution Equivalence of Ordinary/Dynamic Networks)
Let N be an ordinary constraint network over variables $V_1, \ldots, V_m$ and let, for $n \geq m$, $N' = \{C_1, \ldots C_n\}$ be a dynamic constraint network. N and N' are solution equivalent if there is a generating set $M' = \{C_{i_1}, \ldots, C_{i_m}\}$ of N' such that for every solution S of N and every solution S' of N', S equals the restriction of S' to M' up to a permutation of elements.

The definition of solution equivalence is applicable to every pair consisting of an ordinary and a dynamic constraint network. However, we are only interested in

- comparing an ordinary network with a dynamic network that is the translation of the ordinary network and

- comparing a dynamic network with an ordinary network that is a corresponding network of the dynamic network.

You may already have suspected that ordinary and dynamic networks, respectively, are solution equivalent to their translated and corresponding networks, respectively. This is stated in the following propositions:

Prop. 4 (Solution Equivalence of Ordinary/Translated Networks)
Let N be an ordinary constraint network and N' be a dynamic network that is a translation of N, then N and N' are solution equivalent.

Proof: Let $M' \subseteq N'$ consist of the 0-ary dynamic constraints derived from the variables of N. Since M' are the only 0-ary constraints in N', it follows from proposition 1 that M' is a generating set. From that and the definition of a generating set, the proposition follows immediately.
$\square$

Prop. 5 (Solution Equivalence of Dynamic/Corresponding Networks)
Let N' be a dynamic constraint network and let N be its corresponding ordinary constraint network, then N and N' are solution equivalent.

Proof: Let $(d_1, \ldots, d_n)$, $d_i \in D_i$ be a solution of N. Since N is a corresponding network of N', N' consists of dynamic constraints $C'_1, \ldots, C'_n$, where the domain of C'_i is D_i. $N = \{C'_1, \ldots, C'_n\}$ is a generating set of itself. Moreover, by definition of a corresponding network, $(d_1, \ldots, d_n)$ is a solution of N'.
□

These propositions finally show that ordinary and dynamic constraint networks are really equally expressive in theory. Not only that you can transform them syntactically into each other, but the solutions of the respective transformed versions are essentially the same.

3.3 Consistency

While a solution is what you would want to get out of a constraint network, there is an important class of "intermediate" properties of constraint networks: levels of *consistency*. As usual, this family of concepts makes sense in dynamic and in ordinary constraint networks analogously. The idea is that in order to find a solution for the whole network, you assume that you are able to find a solution for some smaller network or networks, thereby reducing the problem, and to make sure that every such partial solution can be extended to a solution of the whole network. Backtracking, as described in chapter 5, is an example for a simple method proceeding in that way. Depending on what portion of the network you assume to be consistent beforehand, there are different levels of consistency.

The basic concept here is "plain" consistency. The idea is that, in a dynamic constraint network consisting of n constraints, any solution for a subnetwork of $(n-1)$ constraints can be completed to a solution of the whole network by choosing an allowed value for the nth constraint. In fact, the following definition is a bit sharper: you need not consider the whole network but only some generating set; by definition, every solution for the generating subnetwork leads to a solution of the whole network. In ordinary networks, you would, of course, just choose values for the variables, i.e., in dynamic constraint network terminology, just take the generating set consisting of all 0-ary constraints. The definition of consistency, then, reads as follows:

Def. 11 (Consistency)
A dynamic constraint network N is consistent w.r.t. a generating set $\{C_1, \ldots, C_m\} \subseteq N$ over domains $D_1, \ldots, D_m$, if for each $j \in \{1, \ldots, m\}$:
every tuple $(d_1, \ldots, d_{j-1}, d_{j+1}, \ldots, d_m)$, $d_i \in D_i$ for all $i \in \{1, \ldots, m\} \setminus \{j\}$, that leads to a solution of $\rho_N(\{C_1, \ldots, C_{j-1}, C_{j+1}, \ldots, C_m\})$ can be extended to an m-tuple $(d_1, \ldots, d_m)$, $d_j \in D_j$, that leads to a solution of $\rho_N(\{C_1, \ldots, C_m\})$.

A few comments are in order. First, the same network can differ in consistency with respect to different generating sets. Take as an example the network in figure 3.4. The network is consistent with respect to the generating set $\{\prec_1, \prec_3\}$; however, it is not

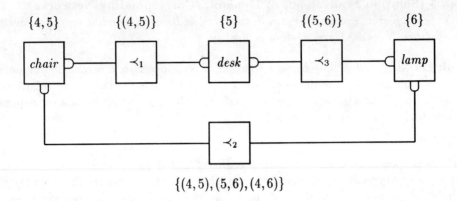

Figure 3.4: A dynamic constraint network consistent w.r.t. $\{\prec_1, \prec_3\}$, but not w.r.t. $\{chair, desk, lamp\}$

consistent with respect to the generating set $G = \{chair, desk, lamp\}$: Take as an $(m-1)$-element subset of G the set $G' = \{chair, lamp\}$; the subnetwork resulting from this set has a solution where $chair = 5$ and $lamp = 6$; this solution, however, cannot be extended to a solution of the whole network.

A second comment: We (and the constraint literature) sometimes speak of *inconsistent* networks with the meaning that such a network has no solution. Note that this notion of inconsistency is *not* the contrary of consistency as defined here! There may be networks that are not inconsistent, i.e., have solutions, that are also not consistent, regarding some of their generating sets. You have already seen an example: the network in figure 3.4 with the generating set G'.

Even more confusing: Some inconsistent networks are consistent! Take as an example an arbitrary, non-empty dynamic constraint network with the domains of all dynamic constraints being empty. This network clearly has no solution, i.e., it is inconsistent; on the other hand, it is trivially consistent because the definition of consistency has the form of an implication, where the premise is constantly wrong in this example. Note that the problem here is not caused by the concepts of consistency and inconsistency, but just by their names; we have adapted these in order to be in accordance—or to be consistent, if you like—with the literature.

As we have already said, consistency is meant to be an "intermediate" concept useful on the way of finding solutions of constraint networks. For this purpose, consistency as defined above is still a bit impractical as it reduces the task only slightly: by reducing the generating sets you have to deal with by only one single dynamic constraint, you don't reduce the problem to solve so much. For fine-tuning the degree of locality to be considered, there is the concept of k-*consistency*, roughly meaning consistency for every sub-network of cardinality k. Here is the exact definition:

Def. 12 (k-**Consistency**)
Let N be a dynamic constraint network, $G = \{C_1, \ldots, C_m\}$ a generating set of N, and

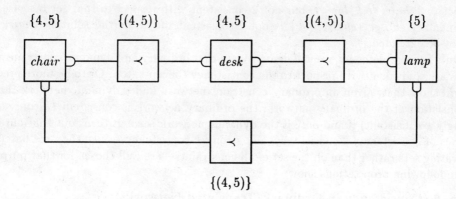

Figure 3.5: A dynamic constraint network that is 2-consistent w.r.t. {*chair*, *desk*, *lamp*} but not w.r.t. the set containing the $\prec$ constraints.

$k \leq m$. *N is k-consistent w.r.t. G if the resulting set of every k element subset M of G is consistent w.r.t. M.*

For historical reasons (see [Mackworth, 1977]), 2-consistency in ordinary networks consisting exclusively of binary constraints is sometimes called *arc consistency*, and the notion of *path consistency* in these networks proves to be equivalent to 3-consistency. We will avoid these names here.

Before we discuss the concept of k-consistency and give examples, let us introduce a sharper form of k-consistency, strong k-consistency:

Def. 13 (Strong k-Consistency)
Let N be a dynamic constraint network, $G = \{C_1, \ldots, C_m\}$ a generating set of N, and $k \leq m$. N is strongly k-consistent w.r.t. G if it is i-consistent w.r.t. G for all $i \leq k$.

Note that, as with consistency, different generating sets may imply different levels of k-consistency, i.e., a network may be, for example, 2-consistent with respect to one generating set but not with respect to another. This is the case in the dynamic network of figure 3.5, which is 2-consistent with respect to {*chair*, *desk*, *lamp*} but not with respect to the set containing the $\prec$ constraints. The reason here is that the resulting set of any two-element subset of {*chair*, *desk*, *lamp*} contains only three dynamic constraints (the elements of the generating set and the dynamic constraint that has these elements as dependents), whereas each two-element set of $\prec$ constraints generates the set of all constraints. Note, moreover, that the network has no solution, i.e., is inconsistent; thus we see what we might have expected: that k-consistency does not imply having a solution.

Strong k-consistency is not a trivial concept. You might think that k-consistency always implies $(k - 1)$-consistency, in which case strong k-consistency *would* be trivial. But this is wrong as you can see by the following example: Take the network in figure 3.5, let the relations of *chair*, *desk*, and *lamp* be {4,6}, {5}, {6}, respectively, and set the relations of all $\prec$ constraints to {(4,5),(4,6),(5,6)}. The network is 3-consistent with respect to $\{chair, desk, lamp\}$, but not 2-consistent with respect to that set because the 2-elementary subset $\{chair, desk\}$ is not 2-consistent. (The partial solution $chair = 6$ cannot be extended.)

Only for completeness, we will demonstrate that ordinary and dynamic constraint networks are equivalent with respect to the consistency concepts, too. Or to be more precise: we will show that, given an ordinary constraint network and a dynamic network that is a translation of the ordinary network, the ordinary network is consistent (k-consistent, strongly k-consistent) if and only if the dynamic network is so. It turns out that our definitions of consistency, k-consistency, and strong k-consistency—since they are based on generating sets rather than on the set of all constraints—are well-chosen for that purpose, as the following propositions show:

Prop. 6 (Consistency in Ordinary/Translated Networks)

Let N be a constraint network involving m variables and N' be a dynamic network that is a translation of N. Then, the following equivalence holds:

$$N \text{ consistent} \iff N' \text{ consistent with respect to } \{C_1, \ldots, C_m\}$$

where $C_1, \ldots, C_m$ are the dynamic constraints of N' that are the translations of the variables of N.

Proof: Let M be the set of variables of N, and let M' be the dynamic constraints that correspond to M. By proposition 1, we know that M' is a generating set of N', i.e., each solution of N' can be reconstructed from a value assignment to M' by combining the values according to the constraints in N. A tuple of values $d_1, \ldots, d_m$ is therefore a solution of N if and only if it leads us to a solution of the resulting set of M', i.e., to a solution of N'. The same holds for every subset $L \subseteq M$ and its corresponding subset $L' \subseteq M'$: a tuple of values is a solution of M if and only if it leads us to a solution of the resulting set of M'. Therefore, the proposition follows immediately.
$\square$

The proofs for k-consistency and strong k-consistency are analogous, and hence we just state:

Prop. 7 (k-Consistency in Ordinary/Translated Networks)

Let N be a constraint network involving m variables and N' be a dynamic network that is a translation of N. Then, the following equivalences hold:

$$N \text{ } k\text{-consistent} \iff N' \text{ } k\text{-consistent w.r.t. } \{C_1, \ldots, C_m\}$$

$$N \text{ strongly } k\text{-consistent} \iff N' \text{ strongly } k\text{-consistent w.r.t. } \{C_1, \ldots, C_m\}$$

where $C_1, \ldots, C_m$ are the dynamic constraints of N' that are the translations of the variables of N.

For reasons of symmetry, we will state analog propositions for the relationships between consistency (k-consistency, strong k-consistency) in dynamic constraint networks and consistency (k-consistency, strong k-consistency) in the corresponding ordinary networks. Since they involve all constraints of the dynamic network as generating sets, these propositions are probably more of a theoretical than a practical value.

Prop. 8 (Consistency in Dynamic/Corresponding Networks)
Let N be a dynamic network consisting of dynamic constraints $C_1, \ldots, C_m$ and N' be a corresponding ordinary constraint network. Then, the following equivalence holds:

$$N \text{ consistent with respect to } \{C_1, \ldots, C_m\} \iff N' \text{ consistent}$$

Proof: Since N' is a corresponding network of N, it contains exactly one variable for each $C_i \in N$, and no other variables. Let $(d_1, \ldots, d_k)$ be a value assignment to a subset M', $|M'| = k$, of variables of N' that is a solution of the subnetwork spanned by M'. Then, $(d_1, \ldots, d_k)$ is also a solution of the network consisting of the dynamic constraints that correspond to M'. The reverse holds as well. From that and the definitions of consistency the proposition follows immediately.
□

Again, the proofs for k-consistency and strong k-consistency are analogous:

Prop. 9 (k-Consistency in Dynamic/Corresponding Networks)
Let N be a dynamic network consisting of dynamic constraints $C_1, \ldots, C_m$ and N' be a corresponding ordinary constraint network. Then, the following equivalences hold:

$$N \text{ } k\text{-consistent w.r.t. } \{C_1, \ldots, C_m\} \iff N' \text{ } k\text{-consistent}$$

$$N \text{ strongly } k\text{-consistent w.r.t. } \{C_1, \ldots, C_m\} \iff N' \text{ strongly } k\text{-consistent}$$

Finally, there is another type of consistency which is related but different to the consistency types presented so far: *local* consistency. The idea is the following: If you look at every dynamic constraint in isolation and take an arbitrary combination of single values for all but one of its dependents, then you must be able to find a value for the remaining dependent such that the whole tuple of values satisfies the constraint. Formally, this is expressed as follows:

Def. 14 (Local Consistency)
A dynamic constraint network N is locally consistent if the following holds for all $C \in N$ with $\delta(C) = \{C_1, \ldots, C_k\}$ and with constraint relations $R, R_1, \ldots, R_k$, respectively, and for all $i \in \{1, \ldots, k\}$:
if $(d_1, \ldots, d_{i-1}, d_{i+1}, \ldots, dk) \in R_1 \times \ldots \times R_{i-1} \times R_{i+1} \times \ldots \times R_k$ then there is $d_i \in R_i$ such that $(d_1, \ldots, d_k) \in R$.

Note that local consistency does not take a generating set into account as the other consistency concepts do.

Assuming that it is *solutions* in what you are really interested concerning dynamic constraint networks, the sense of local consistency as an interesting "intermediate" property of dynamic networks should be clear. Local consistency can be used as a—well—local, i.e., cheap method of checking whether the relations of dynamic constraints in the network contain values that are implausible in the sense that they cannot participate in a tuple of values satisfying some constraint in the network. Because of the importance of local consistency, there is a whole class of algorithms transforming constraint networks into locally consistent ones: the filter algorithms (presented in chapter 6). Note, however, that local

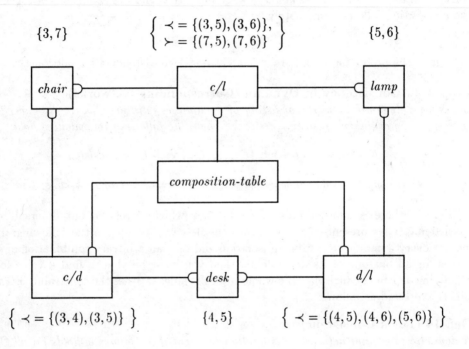

Figure 3.6: Another dynamic constraint network for the office scenario. The relations of the c/l, c/d, and d/l dynamic constraints are given in terms of the spatial relations $\prec, \succ$, where these are given in terms of the respective integer pairs.

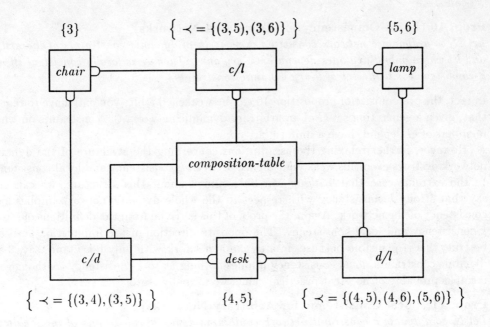

Figure 3.7: A locally consistent dynamic network for the office scenario.

consistency (like the other consistency notions) does not necessarily imply solvability of a network.

As examples for local consistency, consider the dynamic network in figure 3.6. This network is not locally consistent. Take, for example, the *c/d* constraint: for the assignment *chair* = 7, you cannot find appropriate relation elements for *desk* and *c/d* itself. Moreover, for *c/l* = $\succ$ and $\prec$ for one of the *c/d*, *d/l* constraints, respectively, there is no assignment for the third constraint that is sanctioned by *composition-table*(cf. the definition of *composition-table* as given in figure 2.6). However, if the network is modified a little, we get a locally consistent variant of the network in figure 3.6; this variant is shown in figure 3.7.

Let us briefly examine some of the relationships between local consistency on the one hand and *k*-consistency and strong *k*-consistency on the other. These concepts are relatively closely related for ordinary constraint networks—or for translated networks— and relatively unrelated for dynamic constraint networks with arbitrary structure.

To start with, imagine a dynamic network that is a translation of an ordinary one with constraints of uniform arity *k*. That is, the dynamic network consists of 0-ary and *k*-ary dynamic constraints, where only 0-ary ones depend on *k*-ary ones. For such a very special type of dynamic network, local consistency is equivalent to *k*-consistency with respect to the generating set consisting of all 0-ary dynamic constraints. This is obvious because the definitions of *k*-consistency and local consistency essentially coincide in this case. Thus we can state

Prop. 10 (Local Consistency for Translated Networks)
*Let N be a dynamic network consisting exclusively of dynamic constraints of the arity 0
and k, where only 0-ary ones depend on k-ary ones. Then N is locally consistent iff it is
k-consistent w.r.t. the set of 0-ary dynamic constraints.*

In fact, the prerequisite of proposition 10 can be weakened a bit: you only have to require
that, given a generating set G of an arbitrary dynamic network, the constraints on which
members of G depend, have a uniform arity k.

However, further relaxing the assumptions concerning the structure of the dynamic
network destroys even this weak equivalence between k-consistency and local consistency.
In the extreme case that *nothing* can be assumed about this structure, we can only
say that strong k-consistency with respect to the whole dynamic network implies local
consistency of the network. Again, the proof of this is trivial from the definitions of strong
k-consistency and local consistency. The opposite direction of the implication need not
be true; this is plausible because, in a dynamic network with only 0-ary and, say, 3-ary
dynamic constraints, local consistency implies nothing as to 2-consistency. Although the
result is probably of no great practical value, we formally state:

Prop. 11 (Local Consistency for Arbitrary Networks)
*Let N be a dynamic constraint network containing dynamic constraints of the maximum
arity of k. If N is strongly k-consistent w.r.t. itself then it is locally consistent.*

With the definitions presented so far, we have all the basic concepts we need for the rest
of this book. Before actually starting to use them, we make a little detour, presenting two
optional desserts to this chapter dealing with related work, a more detailed presentation
of which, however, lies out of the scope of this text. In section 3.4, we deal with the
relationship between constraints and logic, ending up in a sketch of how what we present
in this whole text fits into the currently hot topic of constraint logic programming; in
section 3.5, we comment on the relationship between dynamic constraints and reflective
systems.

3.4   Related Work: Constraints and Logic

Essentially, an ordinary constraint is defined as a relation on variables. As such, it is
closely related to a predicate in first order logic: At least for finite relations, you can
view an ordinary constraint and a predicate as different syntactical forms of expressing
such a relation. In this section, we will comment on the relationship between constraints
and logic, and we will provide a reference to a relevant subpart of the area of constraint
logic programming. For the rest of this section, we restrict ourselves to first order logic
with finite Herbrand universes, i.e., one of the decidable subclasses of full first order logic,
which we mean by default here when we speak just of logic.

It is easy to map ordinary constraint networks into logic. Take the k-ary ordinary
constraint C on constraint variables $V_1, \ldots, V_k$ over domains $D_1, \ldots, D_k$ with a *finite*
relation R. C can be translated into the logical formula

$$(V_1 = d_{1,1} \wedge V_k = d_{k,1}) \oplus \cdots \oplus (V_1 = d_{1,n_1} \wedge V_k = d_{k,n_k}) \tag{3.2}$$

where $\oplus$ denotes the exclusive or, n_i is the cardinality of D_i, and $d_{i,j} \in D_i$. Note that the constraint variables are mapped to logical constants here. A k-tuple satisfying C obviously corresponds to a disjunct in (3.2) that is true, and vice versa.

An ordinary constraint network N is translated into the conjunction $\mathcal{N}$ of formulae representing the constraints in N, where identical constraint variables are mapped to identical logical constants. Obviously, a solution of N corresponds to a model of $\mathcal{N}$, and vice versa. Another form of translating ordinary constraint networks into logic is given by de Kleer [1989]; his translation looks a bit more complicated because he needs to obtain formulae of a different syntactical form.

To describe the relationship between dynamic constraints and logic constructively and in detail, we would have to proceed in two directions. The first is to describe a translation of *dynamic* (rather than ordinary) constraint networks into logic; the second direction is to describe a translation of an arbitrary logic formula into a dynamic constraint network. We will, however, sketch both directions only briefly, giving the reason for being so sketchy afterwards.

As to translating dynamic constraint networks into logic, you already know all the tools you need. Given an arbitrary dynamic constraint network, build its corresponding ordinary network and translate it into logic as described. There might be a more elegant direct translation of dynamic networks, but this is of no interest here. The point is: dynamic networks have a clear counterpart in logic.

As to the second direction, namely, translating logic formulae into dynamic networks, you might be tempted to go, for example, the following way. Remember that every formula can be transformed into an equivalent one containing only the junctors $\neg$ and $\wedge$, these being a *generative system* of propositional logic. Moreover, note that universal quantifiers can be effectively eliminated in our subclass of first order logic by replacing them by appropriate finite conjunctions of formulae; e.g., $\forall x.P(x)$ with the domain of x being $\{a, b\}$ is replaced by $P(a) \wedge P(b)$. (Alternatively, you may interpret a universally quantified formula as a shorthand for the respective conjunction.) All remaining variables in a formula are interpreted as existentially quantified, and the quantifiers are dropped.

In effect, we only would have to describe how to translate formulae containing $\neg$ and $\wedge$ into dynamic networks. However, even with this simplification, the translation is still tricky. To see an example, consider the negation of a ground atomic formula. In logic, there is a difference between $P(a)$ being derivable from a theory, $\neg P(a)$ being derivable, and both of them being consistent with the theory, i.e, the truth or falsity of $P(a)$ being undetermined. Mapping P into a unary dynamic constraint and the argument into its 0-ary dependent C whose domain contains a, only two states would be possible for a: it is in the relation R of C or not. Interpreting, say, $a \in R$ as a being true, you could not make a difference between a being undetermined or negated, which would result in some form of negation by failure, which would be unwelcome here.

A solution of this problem could be to code both the extension of P and the extension of its negation into the dynamic network, where a being in both extensions means that the truth or falsity of $P(a)$ is undetermined, and a being in none of them means that the formula is inconsistent. (This could be checked by an additional binary dynamic constraint on the extensions of P and its complement.) However, *arbitrary formulae* can appear in negated form; hence dynamic networks may become arbitrarily clumsy when using this way of translating negation.

Instead of proposing a solution to this technical problem or of presenting an alternative approach for tackling the translation problem on the whole, let us think why we wouldn't effectively win anything by solving it, and then turn to more interesting questions:

1. For our subset of first order logic, every formula can trivially be transformed into even an ordinary constraint network. This network consists of one ordinary constraint implementing the formula's truth table, and Boolean variables for every ground atom.

2. Hence, together with the result that dynamic constraint networks can be translated into logic, it is clear that the considered subset of logic and dynamic constraints are equally expressive, in some respect.

3. What we gain from the translation is a one-to-one correspondence between solutions of a dynamic constraint network and models of a logical formula.

4. What we do *not* gain from the translation is a direct dynamic network equivalent to the concept of derivability of logic: you cannot derive new dynamic networks from other dynamic networks.

Of course, we don't want to say that derivability cannot be modeled in dynamic constraints. Derivability is just a relation on formula sets, and if these sets are finite (which they are for our subset of logic modulo equivalence), you can perfectly express them in dynamic constraint networks. If you like, you can force *everything* into the Procrustes bed of dynamic constraints. But there is a perfect formalism for dealing with derivability, namely, logic, and we don't see a good reason to make efforts for mimicing this in dynamic networks in a clumsy way.

However, once you have abandoned the idea that it be useful to rebuild everything in one formalism, you may start to think about how to integrate different formalisms in order to exploit the respective strengths for solving practical problems in common. To give an example from the area of logic, there have been fruitful efforts to separate equality handling procedures like special forms of unification out of general logical calculi in order to build more efficient theorem provers. More general, Bürckert [1991] gives a framework for the idea of combining general and specialized reasoning in logic by introducing RQ-resolution; [Bürckert, 1991] also contains references to work in automated deduction going similar ways. Interesting for our context, Jaffar and Lassez [1987] follow the same idea by suggesting a model for logic programming in which the basic execution steps are based upon determining solvability of constraints and which subsumes pure Prolog as well as programming languages like Prolog II and Prolog with real arithmetic.

An example, making even more obvious that ideas from the area of constraint satisfaction can improve a logic theorem prover, is described in [van Hentenryck, 1989]. To understand the main ideas of this work, it is useful to have a closer look at constraint satisfaction algorithms. Without knowing exactly how such an algorithm works (we will describe that below), it is obvious that its kernel must consist of some procedure for testing whether a constraint C is satisfied or not. The test-for satisfiability procedure may work as follows (cf. definition 8): It receives a tuple of values $d_1, \ldots, d_k$ as input (where k is the arity of C and d_i is in the domain D_i of the ith dependent of C), and checks whether the tuple is an element of the relation R of C or not. In other words, the procedure realizes a k-ary predicate P_C over domains $D_1, \ldots, D_k$.

So far, it is only required that R be decidable, i.e., there is *some* computable function realizing P_C. When putting constraint satisfaction in the context of logic programming, a useful way of implementing P_C is to apply a theorem prover, which, for reasons of practical computational complexity, must not require too complicated proofs. One possibility is to restrict P_C as follows:

1. For all ground terms $d_1, \ldots, d_k$, $P_C(d_1, \ldots, d_k)$ can be verified or falsified very easily.[2]

2. P_C ranges over finite domains $D_1, \ldots, D_k$.

Even with these restrictions, the following questions are still open:

1. Which constraint satisfaction algorithms should be used and extended as described above?

2. How should they be incorporated into theorem proving?

It has been shown that those constraint satisfaction algorithms are useful, which are based on the principle of filtering, i.e., which remove values not satisfying a constraint from its relations. Such algorithms are discussed in detail in chapters 6 and 7. The way they are incorporated into the theorem prover is as follows. When a predicate that fulfills the above requirements occurs in the goal clause of the logical program, the filtering algorithm is invoked, and values not satisfying the constraint are deleted from the domains of the logical variables to which the predicate is applied. This modification of domains is stored and transferred to the theorem prover in form of a substitution that replaces a variable whose domain has been modified by a new variable ranging over the modified domain.

To summarize the essentials of this way of integrating constraint satisfaction and logic programming:

1. A theorem prover can be embedded in a constraint satisfaction algorithm for implementing the test-for-satisfiability procedure. The use of the theorem prover is restricted to such predicates that are easy to verify and to falsify.

2. A constraint satisfaction algorithm can be incorporated into a theorem prover in such a way that it is applied when a special type of predicates occurs. The result of the application is transferred to the theorem prover in form of substitutions.

The area of constraint logic programming includes other techniques and ideas which are broadly different from the ones just described, like linear programming, and which are not part of the classical AI work on constraint reasoning. Hence you will not find them in this text. For references to the whole field of constraint logic programming, see [van Hentenryck, 1989].

---

[2]This is of course only an intuitive definition. For those interested in a formal definition of *to be verified or falsified very easily*, we refer to [van Hentenryck, 1989], where a more formal definition is given in the context of SLD resolution.

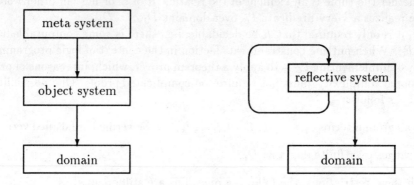

Figure 3.8: Structure of a meta/reflective system.

3.5   Related Work: Reflective Systems

The framework of dynamic constraints enables us to view constraint satisfaction as an even more powerful tool than it was before and to open new perspectives. One of these are reflective systems, a sketch of which we want to serve as the second dessert of this chapter. Some readers may argue that this dessert does not fit into the rest of the menu and that it is better to call for the check now. Even worse, they may even think of it as of marshmallows: nobody knows exactly what they are made of. Don't worry! We use a simple recipe here with natural ingredients only, including no (syntactic) sugar.

According to [Maes, 1987], a reflective system is a special kind of computational system. A computational system consists of

1. a collection of data that represents the domain[3] the system operates on, and

2. a program that describes how to manipulate these data.

A meta system is a computational system whose domain is another computational system, called the object system of the meta system. Maes then defines a reflective system as a meta system whose object system is the meta system itself. This means that the data base of the reflective system contains—besides other information—a representation of the reflective system itself (cf. figure 3.8, where → means *operates on*). A Lisp function, for example, whose body contains statements that change (implicitly) the definition of the function, may be viewed as a simple reflective system.

Reflective systems, or more precisely identifying meta and reflective layers in a computational system, have a practical value for structuring knowledge based systems. See [Voß *et al.*, 1987] for examples (which, by the way, involve constraint relaxation, the topic of the next chapter).

---

[3]The notion of domain is used here in the sense of application area and should not be confused with the domain of a variable or a relation.

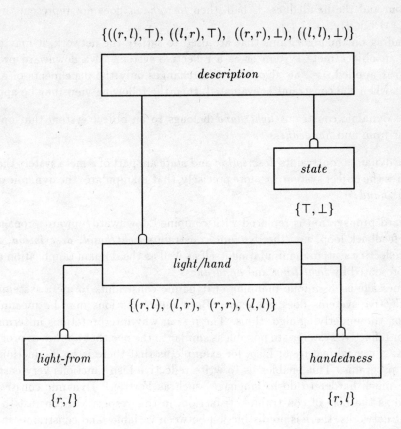

Figure 3.9: A simple reflective network for lighting a desk.

There seems to be a certain relationship between reflective systems and dynamic constraints. Since there is no distinction between variables and constraints, dynamic constraints may be used for the design of reflective constraint systems.

Consider, for example, the simple network shown in figure 3.9, which is supposed to model furnishing a desk with light from a direction depending on the handedness of the person working at that desk. In the case where the desk is lighted adequately, *light-from* is equal to $r(l)$ if and only if *handedness* is equal to $l(r)$.[4] However, if the desk is lighted incorrectly, *light-from* and *handedness* may have the same value. The dynamic constraint *state* reflects whether the desk is lighted in the right way ($\top$) or not ($\bot$). Its values are combined with the values of the dynamic constraint *light/hand*, which results in determining the relation of *description*. If the combination between the direction the light

---

[4]This is, by the way, an example involving spatial reasoning with an *intrinsic* reference frame: The *light-from* constraint represents the position of, say, a window relative to the desk in the intrinsic orientation of the desk.

comes from and the handedness is bad, then *light/hand* does not represent the relation $\{(r,l),(l,r)\}$ but $\{(r,r),(l,l)\}$.

Depending on the algorithms that are used to satisfy the network, it may be viewed either as an object/meta system or as a reflective system. If a downward propagation algorithm is applied, i.e., an algorithm that changes only the dependents of a dynamic constraint when the constraint is evaluated, then the following view may be appropriate:

- The dynamic constraint *light/hand* belongs to an object system that operates on *light-from* and *handedness*.

- The dynamic constraints *description* and *state* are part of a meta system that manipulates the object system, or more precisely, that manipulates the dynamic constraint *light/hand*.

If downward propagation is replaced with combined downward/upward propagation, we obtain a feedback loop, i.e., the dynamic constraints *light/hand*, *description*, and *state* define a reflective system manipulating itself as well as the domain (application area), the latter represented by *light-from* and *handedness*.

The message is: a unique mapping of dynamic constraints to meta systems, respectively reflective systems does not exist. Both interpretations may be meaningful, depending on the underlying algorithms. The reason why interpretations in terms of meta systems or reflective systems are possible is similar to the one that applies to programming languages: a crucial feature of Lisp, for example, is that there is *no* distinction between data and programs. This enables us to write reflective Lisp functions very easily, which would be much harder to do in languages such as Fortran. Dynamic constraints may be viewed as the Lisp of constraint satisfaction, in this respect. In contrast to ordinary constraint networks, there is no distinction between variables and constraints in dynamic networks. Therefore, they are a good candidate for building a reflective system.

Chapter 4

Constraint Relaxation

Soon after the advent of ordinary constraints as a knowledge representation formalism, it turned out that there is a particular problem in using them for representing practical problems: real world problems, when taken literally, tend to be inconsistent. Usually, there are so many features which one would like or even require the solution of a problem to have, that there really *is* no solution—the problem is overspecified.

Motivated by practical applications as described in [Descotte and Latombe, 1985; Borning *et al.*, 1987; Freeman-Benson *et al.*, 1990], an idea developed that has later been called *constraint relaxation* [Dechter and Pearl, 1987]. (Freuder [1989] terms it *partial constraint satisfaction*.)[1] The idea is that in fact not every constraint in a constraint network must be satisfied in what one would accept as a solution of the problem, but that there are more or less "hard" constraints, where the hard ones are required to be satisfied, but the soft ones not necessarily. Or, as Freuder [1989] puts it:

> As AI increasingly confronts real world problems, ... we are increasingly likely
> to encouter situations where, rather than searching for a solution to a problem,
> we must, in a sense, search for a problem we can solve.

We will now see how this idea fits into the framework of dynamic constraints.

There are a few theoretical formulations of constraint relaxation, e.g., [Hertzberg *et al.*, 1988; Freuder, 1989], all of which extend CSPs by—in Freuder's terms—a *problem space* and a *metric*, in one way or another:

- The problem space *PS* includes the original problem; it consists of a set of constraint satisfaction problems over constraint networks with an identical structure plus a

---

[1]Note that we will use the term relaxation in the spirit of this idea throughout the text. However, the term is overloaded; another meaning of relaxation of a CSP is to transform it to an "equivalent" but "simpler" one (where it must be defined what this means in detail) in order to make solving it easier. An example for a relaxation technique in this sense would be filtering as described in chapter 6; texts dealing with relaxation in this interpretation are, for example, [Hummel and Zucker, 1983; Montanari and Rossi, 1991].

partial ordering $\leq$ on them, where for two problems $P, Q \in PS$, $P \leq Q$ is to be interpreted as: P is *weaker* than Q, i.e., every solution of Q is also a solution of P.

- The metric on the problems in *PS* is used to determine a numerical value for the distance between the original problem and a relaxed one.

The idea of a problem space is consistent with the definition of a relaxed constraint in [Dechter and Pearl, 1987]: a constraint is called relaxed if the extension of its relation is a superset of the extension of the original relation.

Solving a CSP now means to find a solution of a relaxed problem in the problem space that is both minimally different, respecting the metric, and only tolerably different from the original problem (where you have to specify what is tolerably different, for example, in terms of a maximal value of the metric).

As an informal example, consider the problem of placing two desks, $desk_1$ and $desk_2$, into an office that has exactly one window; there are the constraints that they be placed face to face and that they both have a window to their left (both desk users are right-handers preferring daylight). Obviously, this problem is unsolvable, when taken literally, and it remains so if you consider all the constraints to be hard. However, interpreting the "face to face" constraint as weak, there is a solution violating this very constraint: both desks are placed with the window on their left, one in front of the other. If, furthermore, the constraint that $desk_1$ have the window on its left is also interpreted as weak and if the metric says that the penalty for violating it is lower than that for violating the *face to face* constraint, then the following solution would be considered optimal: $desk_2$ is placed with the window on its left, and $desk_1$ is placed face to face with it, with the window on its right.

After reading this short example, you might argue that—in contrast to the introduction of this chapter—the problem specification is *not* inconsistent when considering that some of the constraints are weak and may be violated. You are right. As we will see, inconsistency remains inconsistency, even with constraint relaxation, at least in the particular view we describe here. The very idea is in fact not to deal with inconsistency, but to make a difference between hard and—more or less—soft constraints, which may be violated. The enhanced expressivity of using hard and weak constraints just makes it possible to describe solvable problems that would have been inconsistent, i.e., unsolvable, had you described them in terms of uniformly hard constraints.

There is another view of relaxation that really deals with inconsistency and which fits into the general framework given by Freuder. According to this view, you keep the original notion of inconsistent constraint problems, and switch off constraints or add less preferred values to the relation of a constraint in order to resolve the inconsistency. However, there is the following problem in implementing this view directly.

When searching for a solution of a constraint network, one would consider sequences $P_1, P_2, \ldots$ of CSPs or dynCSPs, each P_i being an element of Freuder's problem space. When P_i is considered (because P_{i-1} was still inconsistent), one wants of course to reuse as many of the computations applied to $P_1, \ldots, P_{i-1}$ as possible. However, this is problematical: If you, say, switch off a constraint C after you have seen that P_{i-1} is inconsistent, and if you want to reuse former reasoning steps as far as possible, then you have to withdraw exactly those steps that were based on C being on, all the conclusions drawn from them, and so on. This would require additional mechanisms closely related to those applied in truth maintenance systems; see [Bessière, 1991] as an example.

We will not deal with this issue here, and thus only consider the form of relaxation where in fact no reasoning has to be withdrawn because all the information as to hardness or softness of values is present in the dynamic constraints from the beginning. Looking closer at the two different views of relaxation, you will see that they are not so different in practice. We will deal with this topic neither; see [Brewka *et al.*, 1992] for a discussion.

By the way, besides from being a basis for the view of constraint relaxation we are going to present now, namely navigating around inconsistency, there are more reasons for using differently hard constraints. Intuitively, a weaker problem should be easier to solve, and a solution to it may be found more quickly than a solution for the complete problem. Another purpose of using constraint relaxation may be to find an acceptable— rather than optimal—solution quickly, where what you consider acceptable may vary with the computation time elapsed for searching it.

4.1 Relaxation in Dynamic Networks —The Very Idea

We will now see how constraint relaxation can be handled by dynamic constraints. The idea is to interpret the whole problem space PS as the meta-problem, represent it in a dynamic constraint network, and solve it, resulting in an object-problem plus its solution.

There are different ways to do so. A straightforward one is to represent a weak ordinary constraint with the constraint relation R by two dynamic ones: one constraint expressing R, and another one, depending on the first, representing the information whether the respective relation elements of the first one are relaxed or not; the latter depends on no other constraint and has no dependents itself. In order to do so, we increase the arity of the original relation by one, resulting in a new relation R'; the new argument, which will be the first one, now shows the "mode" of the constraint elements: relaxed ($\perp$) or nonrelaxed ($\top$). We will call these newly introduced *relax-R* constraints *relaxation constraints* henceforth. Using $\bar{x}$ as an abbreviation for $x_1, \ldots, x_k$, in sum, R' is defined by

$$R' = \{(\top, \bar{x}) \mid (\bar{x}) \in R\} \cup \{(\perp, \bar{x}) \mid (\bar{x}) \notin R\}$$

The transformation is shown by figure 4.1.

We have in fact already seen something very similar to this: the dynamic constraint network we used to discuss the idea of reflective systems, cf. figure 3.9. To be in full accordance with the pattern given in figure 4.1, we change the representation a bit and obtain the dynamic constraint mini-network shown in figure 4.2.

This relaxation schema works perfectly for ordinary networks or for relaxing the non-0-ary dynamic constraints in dynamic networks that are translations of ordinary ones. For dynamic networks in general, however, there are some problems. First, note that the schema as described works only for constraints with dependents. A 0-ary dynamic constraint C with relation R would have to be promoted to a 2-ary one C' with the relation R' as described, and you have to introduce *two* additional ones, namely, the *relax* constraint and another 0-ary one with the old relation R as a dependent of C'.

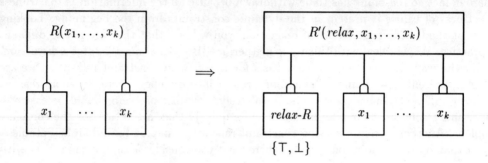

Figure 4.1: Transforming a dynamic constraint to a different one with relaxation.

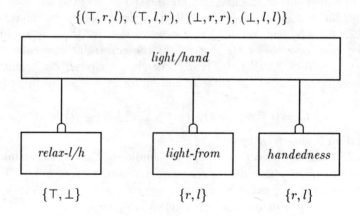

Figure 4.2: Another formulation of the lighting problem using a *relax* constraint.

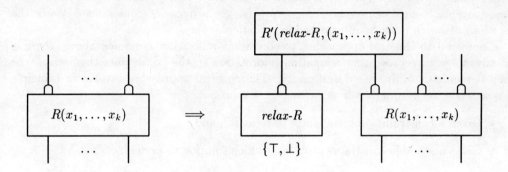

Figure 4.3: Another schema for relaxing a dynamic constraint.

Moreover, the changes in the dynamic network are by far not as local in the constraints to be relaxed as our description might have suggested. After changing the relation R of the constraint C to become R', you have to update the *types* of all relations of all dynamic constraints which C is a dependent of, and recursively upward. This is no serious problem, but both these little technical problems may make the relaxation schema as described a little clumsy for introducing relaxation in dynamic networks of arbitrary structure.

For these cases, there is another relaxation schema that is more appropriate. The idea is to leave the dynamic constraint to be relaxed as it was and to plug a relaxation mechanism on top of it. More exactly: For a dynamic constraint C with its n-ary relation R of domain D, define the relaxed, 2-ary relation R' of type $\{\top, \bot\} \times D$, and introduce a new, 2-ary constraint C' of which C and a newly introduced relaxation constraint are the dependents. Obviously, R' is defined nearly as before:

$$R' = \{(\top; (\bar{x})) \mid (\bar{x}) \in R\} \cup \{(\bot, (\bar{x})) \mid (\bar{x}) \notin R\}$$

The result of transforming a dynamic constraint according to this new schema is shown in figure 4.3.

You still have to change the *relations* of dynamic constraints to be relaxed and to update the relations of the constraints they depend on, recursively, when introducing relaxation into a dynamic network *post hoc*. But this lies in the nature of relaxation, not in this particular schema. Note that the *types* of all formerly existing constraints in the dynamic network stay as they were and that this schema handles dynamic constraints of all arities uniformly.

For this relaxation schema, you actually have seen an example, namely, the original dynamic network for the desk lighting example in figure 3.9. Just change the names of the constraints *description* to *light/hand'* and *state* to *relax-light/hand*.

When interpreting a solution of a dynamic constraint network containing relaxation constraints (regardless of the schema according to which they were introduced), keep in mind that these must be interpreted in the right way: they act and only act as a relevance toggle for their parent dynamic constraints, indicating whether their values are in accordance with their "proper" relation or not. Note that we don't have to introduce new concepts to deal with relaxation. We just get a dynamic constraint network the solutions of which must be interpreted in a particular way.

Compared to classical approaches to constraint relaxation as named above, there is an advantage in representing relaxation information in the constraints themselves—be they dynamic or ordinary—: uniformity. The classical approaches involve in principle two separate decision points in searching for a solution:

- Given a constraint problem—how to relax it?, and

- Given a solvable constraint problem—which solution to prefer?,

the first decision corresponding to a transition from one problem to another in the problem space.

This decision is now reduced to one of the second type: There may be lots of solutions of a dynamic constraint problem; some of them may be interpreted as involving constraint relaxations; and as usual, the constraint satisfaction algorithm used must decide when to stop the process of generating new solutions. Consequently, we can use the standard constraint satisfaction algorithms (for dynamic networks) to do in a relatively intuitive way what we can interpret as constraint relaxation.

Obviously, the decision as to whether some solution is acceptable would involve the metric on the problem space we talked of earlier, and we are now going to discuss it. Obviously, there is not *the* metric, but which one you use heavily depends on the problem at hand. Assuming that constraint relaxation is treated in the simple way just described for dynamic constraint networks, the metric between the original problem P and another one Q could be the number of relaxation constraints taking the value $\{\bot\}$ in Q, but $\{\top, \bot\}$ or $\{\top\}$ in P, i.e., you simply count the dynamic constraints switched off.

In many cases, this proves to be too simple as one would like to make a difference not only between hard and soft, i.e., relaxable constraints, but also state that relaxing different constraints yields different penalties; moreover, there may be different penalties for different variable bindings of the same constraint. To model this, we must first allow the relaxation constraints to be more expressive than they are now.

The idea is that the domain of a relaxation constraint are the nonnegative integers, 0 indicating that the relation is optimally fulfilled and $n > 0$ indicating a more or less severe penalty for the tuples involved. Of course, these values must replace the values $\top, \bot$ in the "proper" dynamic constraint, too. The metric, then, can be constructed as a function in the values of the relaxation constraints. (This works in a straightforward way for defining a metric on *solutions* rather than dynamic constraint *problems* in general, but we will consider measuring solutions only.) Let us show all this by an example.

4.2   An Example

The example is determining the relative positions of a window, a desk, a terminal table, and a bookcase in the corner of an office. That seems pretty simple, and we will simplify matters even more by fixing the relationship between desk and window. We will see in a

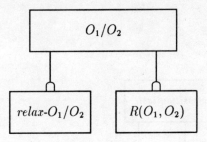

Figure 4.4: A relaxable constraint for the relative positions of two objects.

minute, however, that the full example would in fact be breathtakingly complex, and so we will restrict it a bit.

A constraint representing the relative position between two of the involved objects, O_1 and O_2, will be represented as shown in figure 4.4. The *relax* constraint cares for the relaxation information; the R constraint handles the 2-dimensional spatial relation between the objects involved. They will in principle enumerate all the possible relation pairs for the x and y components in the form described in section 2.3.

In the full example, there would have to be an instance of the 2-dimensional version of the composition table constraint between every triple of $O_1/O_2, O_1/O_3, O_2/O_3$ constraints. We assume they are present, but for simplicity mostly omit them in the discussions and sketches to follow. The topology of the resulting constraint network is shown in figure 4.5.

Let us then look at the objects to be placed. A sketch of the office corner to be furnished is given in figure 4.6. We are only interested in the part of the whole room that is shown; in fact, we assume the room to be arbitrarily large. The position of the desk is fixed in front of the window. Note that the terminal table has no intrinsic orientation and that the bookcase is longer and narrower than the desk.

Obviously, a window, a desk, and a bookcase have (intrinsic) orientations: as we have discussed in chapter 3, it makes sense to talk of *left of the desk,* independent of its (deictic) orientation with respect to fixed space axes. To circumvent this problem, we again make the convention that *left of the desk* is represented as $\prec$ or $\preceq$ in the x component, which is in accordance with the orientation of the desk in figure 4.6. We will not need the orientation of the window, and the orientation of the bookcase will be dealt with differently.

Now, let us turn to the actual relations of the constraints. First of all, there are inter-object relations that are definitely not allowed for windows, desks, shelves, and tables:[2]

- Objects overlapping or containing each other in both x and y direction, e.g., $\langle \Leftarrow, \sqsupset \rangle$ or $\langle \Rightarrow, \Rightarrow \rangle$.

- A bookcase occluding a window (which, in our example, is subsumed by the previous item).

---

[2]In general, there are more combinations of objects that must be forbidden than those expressible by local inter-object relations. For example, each object in an office should be freely accessible: this is a constraint on *all* objects involved. We will not model such constraints in our example. (Even more: we wouldn't propose to model such a condition by constraints at all.)

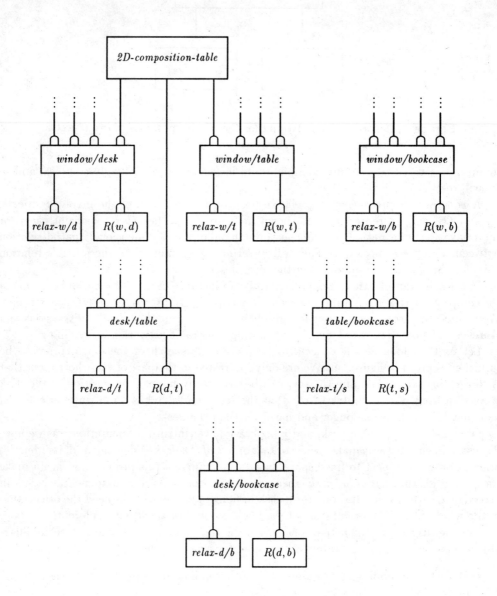

Figure 4.5: Sketch of the dynamic network for the example problem.

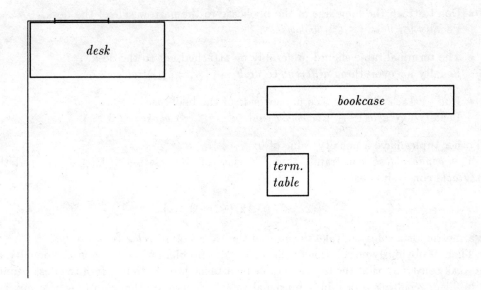

Figure 4.6: A sketch of the relaxable office corner furnishing problem.

- Objects directly in front of the desk; regarding our direction convention for the desk, these are objects $\preceq$ the desk in y direction.

- In this particular example, nothing to the left and nothing behind the desk and nothing behind the window is allowed.

As we will explicitly enumerate all the inter-object relations to be considered for two objects in the respective constraint, there is a very simple way to exclude these relations: they are simply omitted in the enumeration.

Finally, let us turn to what is really of concern here: the relaxable constraints. We will state a couple of these that are relevant for our example; we will also say something about the penalties resulting from violating them. Obviously, these are somewhat arbitrary.

- Don't attach the long side of the bookcase to the narrow side of the desk.
  Penalty for *desk* $\langle \preceq, \sqsubset \rangle$ *bookcase*: 5

- The terminal table should preferably be attached left to the desk.
  Penalty for everything *different* to *desk* $\langle \succ, \{\succ, \Rightarrow, \sqsupset\} \rangle$ *table*: 2

- Don't attach the table to a narrow side of the bookcase.
  Penalty for *table* $\langle \preceq, \sqsubset \rangle$ *bookcase* and *table* $\langle \sqsubset, \preceq \rangle$ *bookcase*: 3

All other tuples have a penalty value of 0.

The *window/desk* constraint, then, consists of the relation $\{(0, \langle \sqsubset, \succ \rangle)\}$, and the *desk/table* constraint reads

$$\{(2, \langle \prec, \sqsupset \rangle), (2, \langle \prec, \Rightarrow \rangle), \ldots\}$$

As a metric for a solution, take the sum of the values of all *relax* constraints.

There is obviously no solution of this constraint problem without a nonzero penalty, as the weak constraint that the terminal table be attached to the front left of the desk cannot be fulfilled, resulting in a minimum penalty of 2. There are, however, a whole number of solutions to this problem. Restricting them to the really interesting relations between *desk*, *table*, and *bookcase* (the relations with respect to *window* are straightforward), two of these solutions are

1. *desk/bookcase* : $(5, \langle \preceq, \sqsubset \rangle)$
    table/bookcase : $(3, \langle \sqsupset, \preceq \rangle)$
    desk/table : $(2, \langle \Leftarrow, \succ \rangle)$

2. *desk/bookcase* : $(0, \langle \sqsubset, \succ \rangle)$
    table/bookcase : $(0, \langle \sqsubset, \succ \rangle)$
    desk/table : $(2, \langle \preceq, \sqsupset \rangle)$

The solutions are depicted in figure 4.7. Using the given metric, the solutions have penalties of 10 and 2, respectively, so the second solution would be preferred.

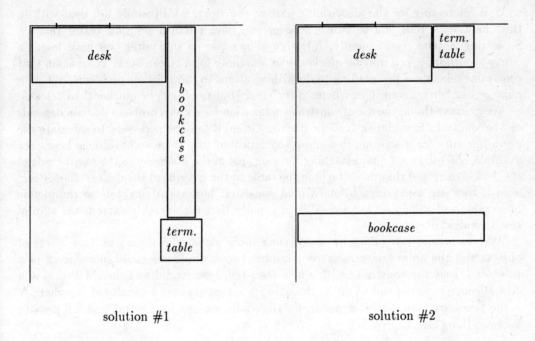

solution #1   solution #2

Figure 4.7: Two solutions of the relaxable office corner furnishing problem.

4.3   More about the Metric

Not only when in explicit search for a quick solution but also when searching an acceptable solution, it may prove useful not to head for one with a globally minimal penalty. However, we must specify what acceptable means here; of course we have to do so in terms of the overall penalty of a solution. Following Freuder [1989], we introduce necessary and sufficient bounds (N, S), $S \leq N$, on the metric with the obvious interpretation that we would not accept a solution with a penalty greater than N and we would accept every solution with a penalty less than or equal to S.[3] Setting N too tight may result in an unsolvable problem, as does $N = 1$ in our example. $N = 0$ always results in a non-relaxable problem.

S is interesting for the algorithmic part of the story, which we do not deal with in this chapter: it tells you to stop whenever you have found a solution better than S. So setting S (and, consequently, N) large allows you to stop after you have found a "dirty" solution, which may be quicker than searching for a "clean" one. Note again that constraint relaxation has nothing to do with solutions to inconsistent problems, but with more or less "dirty" solutions, where "dirty" may (but need not) be quicker than "clean".

As you may think, the use of constraint relaxation for a given problem domain depends on the ability to formulate a realistic metric. Often, it may be necessary to calculate the overall penalty for a solution in a more sophisticated way than we have done here. For example, one might say that attaching the long side of the bookcase to the narrow side of the desk is okay and that not attaching the table to the left side of the desk is okay either, even if they are sanctioned by individual penalties; however, doing *both* is completely intolerable and should be sanctioned by a penalty that considerably exceeds the sum of the individual ones.

We can model this easily by introducing more global constraints on larger sets of objects and the appropriate *relax* constraints. For example, we could introduce a new *table/desk/bookcase* constraint with a new *relax-t/d/b* constraint and the old $R(d, b)$ and $R(d, t)$ constraints depending on it. It would state that there is a penalty of N, where N is the necessary bound on the metric, for the configurations in question and a 0 penalty for everything else, i.e.,

$$\{(N, \langle \preceq, \sqsubset \rangle, \langle \succ, \succ \rangle), (N, \langle \preceq, \sqsubset \rangle, \langle \succ, \Rightarrow \rangle), \ldots, (0, \langle \prec, \prec \rangle, \langle \prec, \prec \rangle), \ldots\}$$

The modified metric respecting the new *relax* constraint would, for example, yield a penalty of $N + 10$ to the first solution given in the previous section, leaving the penalty of the second solution given as it was.

There is a particular metric—which has been used in [Descotte and Latombe, 1985] and more theoretically examined in [Hertzberg et al., 1988]—that seems to be relatively intuitive, which is why we want to briefly present it as another approach to (ordinary) constraint relaxation that is subsumed by our framework for relaxation in dynamic constraint networks. The idea is:

- the only form of relaxation of constraints is deactivation;

---

[3]Freuder [1989] in fact defines N and S as bounds on the metric distance between the orginal problem P and an arbitrary solvable problem from the problem space PS. We are a bit more special here.

- there is a partial order on constraints, dividing the constraints in levels; let a constraint of level i be more important than another of level j for $i < j$;

- relaxing any number of constraints of level $i + 1$ is preferred to relaxing one single constraint of level i;

- relaxing different numbers of constraints of the same index yields the same penalty.

Formally writing down a function for modeling an equivalent metric in the framework of dynamic constraints is straightforward for finite dynamic constraint networks, but it is clumsy; so we omit that. (One possibility involves index functions signalling whether there are constraints of index i that have been relaxed.)

This metric is interesting because it is very simply hard-wired into a constraint relaxation procedure that can be sketched as follows:

1. start with the constraint sub-problem involving only the lowest index (i.e., the one signalling highest importance);

2. find a solution of the recent constraint problem, relaxing arbitrary constraints of the presently highest index, if necessary;

3. if the presently highest index is the globally highest index, then stop;
   else add the constraints of the next-highest index to the recent constraint problem, and continue with 2.

As implementation issues are only dealt with in later chapters, we do not want to go into details here. We also do not intend to presume that this approach to relaxation and the metric it involves are particularly clever—it is just one special approach that has received some amount of attention and that has some pleasant formal properties, at least for filtering approaches to (ordinary) constraint satisfaction, see [Hertzberg *et al.*, 1988]. If we were to use this metric in the context of relaxation with dynamic constraints, it would be very simple to include information about how many constraints of the same index are relaxed and preferring solutions that only relax minimally many constraints of each index.

The point is: which metric you use depends on which results you want to get, and finding a good metric remains the cue for arriving at practically good solutions. Hence we want to conclude with a sceptical quote from Freuder [1989]:

> *Computing such a metric, however, is not likely to be easy.*

4.4 Related Work: Nonmonotonic Logical Reasoning

To sum up the results of this chapter, we see that constraint relaxation, at least in the way presented here, has lost the creative flavor of the everyday jumping to a solution of an unsolvable problem by effectively changing it. On the contrary, every conceivable relaxation of a given problem P must be included in the respective problem space PS.

The task is to find a problem $Q \in PS$ that meets given acceptability—or, if you like, optimality—criteria formulated in terms of the metric.

This task is paralleled in a particular subproblem in nonmonotonic reasoning, which we want to sketch here. Of course, we do not want to introduce nonmonotonic reasoning; we assume a basic understanding of what it is and refer the interested reader to [Brewka, 1991] for a detailed introduction.

First of all, note that the general problem of (an aspect of) nonmonotonic reasoning is similar to the one that has led us to considering constraint relaxation: some given set of facts, when expressed in classical predicate logic would be inconsistent, and one tries to qualify a subset of these facts as "weak" facts: defaults. To quote Brewka [1991, page 64]:

> *What makes a piece of knowledge* default *knowledge? What distinguishes it from a fact? Mainly, our attitude towards it in the case of a conflict, that is in the case of an inconsistency. If we take this view seriously then the idea of default reasoning as a special case of inconsistency handling seems quite natural.*

Consider the following example.[4] There is the fact that a certain object L is a lamp, in short

$$lamp(L)$$

Moreover, we have the *default* information that in an office, lamps are normally placed on desks, in short[5]

$$\text{default} : lamp(x) \rightarrow ondesk(x) \tag{4.1}$$

From this information, we would have to conclude that L is placed on the desk, in short

$$ondesk(L)$$

We now get the information that L actually is *not* placed on the desk. Is that compatible with our knowledge? Sure, because the information that lamps are typically placed on the desk is just *default* information; it is defeasible, and it is defeated by the additional information. So,

$$\neg ondesk(L)$$

is consistent with what we know.

Just to state the issue more clearly, we will define what a *scenario* is, i.e., a set of ground fromulas that reasonably follow in a logical theory $\Theta = \Phi \cup \Delta$ from a set of facts, Φ, and a set of defaults, Δ. (We borrow from Poole's [1988] approach to default reasoning here.)

> *A scenario of Φ and Δ is a consistent set $\Delta' \cup \Phi$ where Δ' is a set of ground instances of elements of Δ.*

---

[4]A note for those knowledgeable in default reasoning: the example is isomorphic to the standard Nixon example.

[5]Think of the formula 4.1 as a schema representing all of its ground instances. There is an important difference between quantified and free variables in the approach used here, but we omit that.

The similarity between constraint relaxation and default reasoning can then be stated more clearly: hard constraints correspond to the set Φ of facts, soft constraints correspond to the set Δ of defaults, and the solution to a constraint satisfaction problem corresponds to a scenario of Φ and Δ.[6] As there may be different solutions to a relaxable constraint satisfaction problem, differing in which constraints are relaxed, there may be, in general, different scenarios of a default theory, differing in which defaults have been applied.

Consider as an extension of the lamp example the additional information that L is a floor lamp,

$$floorlamp(L),$$

and another default, which is to be used additionally to default 4.1:

$$default : floorlamp(x) \rightarrow \neg ondesk(x) \tag{4.2}$$

If we are not explicitly informed about L's position, there are two arguments with conflicting outcomes:

1. It may be placed on the desk because it is a lamp, and lamps are typically placed on desks (default 4.1).

2. It may be not placed on the desk because it is a floor lamp, and floor lamps are typically not placed on desks (default 4.2).

Analogously to the need of specifying a metric on the problem space in constraint relaxation, you have to specify which ones among a set of conflicting defaults to prefer in default reasoning.[7] There is an extension of Poole's approach to default reasoning that is well comparable to the constraint relaxation ideas exposed in this chapter: Brewka's [1991, chapter 5] preferred subtheories.

The idea is to make no difference in principle between hard facts and defaults but simply to order subsets of the whole theory Θ at hand linearly, i.e.,

$$\Theta = \Theta_1 \cup \cdots \cup \Theta_n,$$

where the Θs with a lower index are interpreted as being more important than the ones with a higher index. Θ is then called a *level default theory*. (Note that the old definition $\Theta = \Phi \cup \Delta$ is a special case of a level default theory.) We can then define the analog of scenarios:

Let $\Theta = \Theta_1 \cup \cdots \cup \Theta_n$ be a level default theory. $\Theta' = \Theta'_1 \cup \cdots \cup \Theta'_n$ is a preferred subtheory of Θ iff for all k $(1 \leq k \leq n)$, $\Theta'_1 \cup \cdots \cup \Theta'_k$ is a maximal consistent subset of $\Theta_1 \cup \cdots \cup \Theta_k$

---

[6]Well, the scenario should probably be maximal in the sense of set inclusion, and one could argue that everything that logically follows from a scenario should also be included, yielding Poole's concept of an *extension*. We skip this here for brevity.

[7]Not all formalizations of default reasoning go that way. There are default logics incorporating the view that only facts are credible that are contained in *every* scenario (or whatever the analogs to scenarios are in the respective logics); in the lamp example, such logics would simply derive nothing as to L's position as there is conflicting evidence. See [Brewka, 1991] for the details.

Consider two alternative formulations of the lamp example. The first one is in fact the old two-level formulation:

$$\Theta_1 = \{lamp(L), floorlamp(L)\}$$
$$\Theta_2 = \{lamp(x) \rightarrow ondesk(x), floorlamp(x) \rightarrow \neg ondesk(x)\}$$

In analogy to the old formulation, there is a preferred subtheory containing the formula $ondesk(L)$, and another containing $\neg ondesk(L)$. Now look at an alternative formulation, expressing that the property of being a floor lamp is more relevant for the position than the one of being a lamp in general:

$$\Theta_1 = \{lamp(L), floorlamp(L)\}$$
$$\Theta_2 = \{floorlamp(x) \rightarrow \neg ondesk(x)\}$$
$$\Theta_3 = \{lamp(x) \rightarrow ondesk(x)\}$$

There is no preferred subtheory containing Θ_3, so it is derivable that L is not on the desk, as expected.

With regard to what we have learnt about constraint relaxation, we see that the preferred subtheories approach is closely analog to relaxation with a particular metric wired in: satisfy/include as many constraints/formulas of level n before satisfying/including the ones of level $n + 1$. As you should remember, this is just the constraint ordering approach of [Descotte and Latombe, 1985; Hertzberg *et al.*, 1988] we have been talking of at the end of the previous section.

Chapter 5

Backtracking Approaches

As constraint satisfaction is not a new field of AI, a variety of algorithms related to constraint satisfaction have already been developed. They can be used for solving constraint satisfaction problems (including constraint relaxation as described in chapter 4) or for preparing a given problem such that it can be solved more easily (transforming it into a smaller problem by making it, for example, k-consistent). It would not be helpful to introduce really all of these algorithms in this text; thus, we will restrict ourselves to a set of representatives, hoping that these are sufficient to obtain an impression of how dynamic constraint satisfaction problems may be approached.

Constraint satisfaction algorithms may be categorized under different aspects. These aspects are independent of each other, or at least *almost* independent. One aspect is to determine the degree of consistency the algorithms compute, leading to a categorization scheme similar to the scheme introduced in [Freuder, 1978]. A second aspect, which may be inspired by the statistical results described in [Dechter and Meiri, 1989], is to use the efficiency of the algorithms applied to a set of randomly generated constraint satisfaction problems. A third aspect would be the general machine architecture the algorithms are intended or suited for: one-processor machines, machines with a limited number of processors, or massively parallel or connectionist machines.

We will apply none of these aspects to organize the rest of this text. Instead, we structure this and the following three chapters along a functional dimension: what the respective algorithms are good for in constraint-based reasoning. In this chapter, we start with backtracking approaches, which are good for finding a solution for a dynamic constraint network. After that (in chapter 6), we discuss filtering approaches, which are generally used as preprocessing tools for, e.g., backtracking, but which can, as we will see, also find solutions by their own. Finally (in chapter 8), we describe optimization approaches, which are suited for finding good or even optimal solutions.

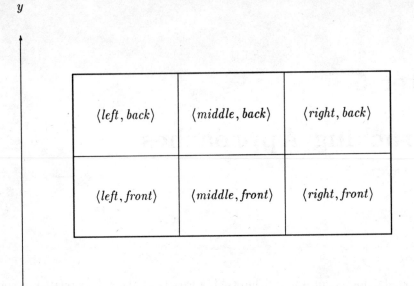

Figure 5.1: A desk with six areas where items may be placed.

5.1   A Brute Force Approach: Chronological Backtracking

A standard approach to finding a solution of a given constraint satisfaction problem is backtracking, the idea of which may be illustrated by an example as follows. Suppose you want to put utensils onto your desk such that certain constraints like *The lamp must be to the left of the computer* and *The phone must be to the right of the computer* are satisfied. Then, you could approach this problem by selecting a utensil, putting it somewhere, testing the constraints, selecting another utensil, and so on. Whenever you come to a point where some constraints are violated, you have to remove some of the utensils that have already been placed on the desk.

Let us consider, for example, a desk which has been divided into six areas as shown in figure 5.1. Instead of characterizing the objects' positions by integers (as in the examples of chapter 3), we use mnemonic values here, for which we assume the following ordering:

$$x\text{-axis:}\quad left \prec middle \prec right$$
$$y\text{-axis:}\quad front \prec back$$

We can now represent the propositions *The lamp must be to the left of the computer* and *The phone must be to the right of the computer* by a simple dynamic network such as the one sketched in figure 5.2. Applying a backtracking algorithm to this network may result in the sequence of assignments shown in figure 5.3.

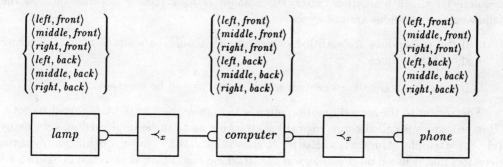

Figure 5.2: Constraint network for the desk example.

Start:	$lamp \leftarrow \langle middle, front \rangle$
Next assignment:	$phone \leftarrow \langle right, front \rangle$
Next assignment:	$computer \leftarrow \langle left, front \rangle$
Inconsistency, choose alternative for *lamp* and keep all other assignments:	$lamp \leftarrow \langle left, back \rangle$
Inconsistency, choose alternative for *computer* and keep all other assignments:	$computer \leftarrow \langle middle, back \rangle$
Solution found:	$lamp = \langle left, back \rangle$ $computer = \langle middle, back \rangle$ $phone = \langle right, front \rangle$

Figure 5.3: Assignments of values to dynamic constraints performed by a backtracking algorithm.

In the example, only two inconsistent situations occurred, and backtracking had to be performed only twice. This is not the case in general. Given a constraint satisfaction problem for which a solution exists, the amount of backtracking depends on how the following two questions are answered:

1. If the constraints are satisfied, which utensil should be selected next, and where should it be placed?

2. If some constraints are violated, which utensil should be removed?

The answer to the second question often is to remove the utensil placed most recently. This procedure is called chronological backtracking and can be implemented very easily (cf., for example, [Guesgen, 1989a]). A constraint satisfaction algorithm for dynamic networks that is based on chronological backtracking might look as sketched in figure 5.4.[1] The algorithm successively assigns values to the dynamic constraints of the generating set and stores these assignments in A. When A becomes inconsistent, then backtracking is performed. The backtracking component of the algorithm tries to delete assignments until a dynamic constraint C_j is found for which alternative assignments $(S_j \neq \emptyset)$ are possible. If no alternatives exist, then the algorithm fails.

If $R_1, \ldots, R_m$ are finite relations, then the sets of candidates for possible assignments, $S_1, \ldots, S_m$, are finite and the algorithm eventually terminates. It is not required that all relations in the dynamic network are finite to guarantee termination. The restriction to those of the generating set is sufficient.

Whether or not a solution can be determined only depends on whether or not a solution exists for the given network. It does not depend on which constraint is selected in step 4a and which value is chosen for this constraint in step 4b. However, which solution is computed does depend on the selections made in steps 4a and 4b, and so does the amount of backtracking that is needed to find a solution.

5.2   Improving Chronological Backtracking

In general, chronological backtracking is not efficient, since, in terms of our example, utensils are removed that are not directly involved in the conflict. To avoid this, an alternative has been developed: dependency-directed backtracking (cf., for example, [Stallman and Sussman, 1977], instances of which are backjumping [Gaschnig, 1979] and graph-based backjumping [Dechter, 1990]. The key idea of dependency-directed backtracking is to examine the current situation and to determine those utensils that caused the conflict. As a result, the algorithm becomes more informed and unnecessary backtracking is eliminated. In the case of graph-based backjumping, the algorithm retracts the value of the most recently set constraint among those connected to the constraint with which the inconsistency was detected. R. Dechter [1990] has shown that graph-based backjumping outperforms backtracking on an instance-by-instance basis without trade-offs, and that the improvement is significant when the constraint graph is sparse.

---

[1]In step 4d of the algorithm, the assignments of a stack A are tested for inconsistency. This means the following: let $(C_1, \ldots, C_k)$ be the constraints stored in A and $(d_1, \ldots, d_k)$ their respective assignments, then the assignments are inconsistent with respect to a given dynamic network N, if $(d_1, \ldots, d_k)$ does not generate a solution of $\rho_N(\{C_1, \ldots, C_k\})$.

Algorithm 1 (Chronological Backtracking)
Given a dynamic constraint network N and a generating set $N_g \subseteq N$ consisting of constraints $C_1, \ldots, C_m$ with relations $R_1, \ldots, R_m$, respectively.

1. *Let A be an empty stack with the usual* pop *and* push *operations.*

2. *Let finished, M, and $S_1, \ldots, S_m$ be appropriate variables.*

3. *Initialize:* $M \leftarrow N_g$
   $$\forall i \in \{1, \ldots, m\} : S_i \leftarrow R_i$$

4. **while** $M \neq \emptyset$ **do**

   (a) *Select a constraint $C_i \in M$ and remove C_i from M, i.e., $M \leftarrow M \setminus \{C_i\}$*

   (b) *Select a value $d \in S_i$ and remove d from S_i, i.e., $S_i \leftarrow S_i \setminus \{d\}$*

   (c) $\text{push}((C_i, d), A)$

   (d) **if** *the assignments in A are inconsistent,* **then do**

       finished $\leftarrow$ **false**

       $(C_j, d') \leftarrow \text{pop}(A)$

       $M \leftarrow M \cup \{C_j\}$

       if *A is empty* **then** *stop algorithm* **and** *return failure*

       if $S_j = \emptyset$ **then** $S_j \leftarrow R_j$ **else** *finished* $\leftarrow$ **true**

       until *finished*

5. *Return A*

Figure 5.4: An algorithm for chronological backtracking in dynamic networks.

Both chronological and dependency-directed backtracking are methods that are applied *after* the occurrance of a conflict. Opposed to that, there are other methods that are applied *before* the occurrance of a conflict. These methods are look-ahead techniques on the one hand, and, on the other hand, **heuristics that control the selections in steps 4a and 4b**, which means in our example: they determine which utensil is to be selected next and where it is to be placed.

Let us first discuss the application of look-ahead techniques. Incorporating them into a backtracking algorithm is straightforward:

1. Replace step 4c of the backtracking algorithm with the following two operations, which, in addition to the original step, save the current constraint relations, and substitute tighter relations for them:

$$\text{push}((C_i, d, S_1, \ldots, S_m), A)$$
$$(S_1, \ldots, S_m) \leftarrow \text{look-ahead}(S_1, \ldots, S_m)$$

2. Extend the pop operation in step 4d such that it restores the previous constraint relations:

$$(C_j, d', S_1, \ldots, S_m) \leftarrow \text{pop}(A)$$

The function look-ahead takes the current dynamic network and transforms it into an equivalent one whose relations are subsets of the original ones. As a result, arc consistency, path consistency, or some higher level of k-consistency is obtained. The methods that are used to get these result may be, for example, forward checking [Haralick and Elliott, 1980] or Waltz filtering as introduced in chapter 3. Dechter and Meiri [1989] found out that, disregarding heuristics for controlling the selection of constraints and values, backtracking combined with a variant of Waltz filtering, namely DAC (Directional Arc Consistency), is the most efficient approach for most constraint problems.

Let us assume that look-ahead performs Waltz filtering, then the desk example given by figures 5.1 and 5.2 may look as shown in figure 5.5.

Though there is much more to say, we will finish our discussion of look-ahead techniques with that example; the interested reader may refer to [Dechter and Meiri, 1989] to obtain an overview and more details. Instead, we will now summarize some of the heuristics that can be used to improve the selection of constraints and values in steps 4a and 4b of the backtracking algorithm introduced above.

Regarding the question of which dynamic constraint of the generating set to select next, it is often advantageous to choose the constraint that cuts the search space maximally. Therefore, the constraint with the highest connectivity should be selected (cf. for example, [Purdom, 1983; Stone and Stone, 1986; Zabih and McAllester, 1988]). Closely related to this is a heuristic that uses the concept of minimal width [Freuder, 1982] as a criterion for selecting the most appropriate constraint. The idea of the minimal width heuristic is to postpone those constraints that are connected only to a few other constraints. The heuristic can be realized by determining the width of a generating set, which is obtained by minimizing the widths of its orderings, which in turn are gained by maximizing the widths of the constraints. The width of a constraint with respect to an ordering is the number of previous constraints in the ordering that are connected to the constraint. An ordering of the generating set is optimal with respect to the heuristic, if

Start:
$$lamp \leftarrow \langle middle, front \rangle$$

Waltz filtering:
$$S_{phone} \leftarrow \emptyset$$
$$S_{computer} \leftarrow \emptyset$$

Inconsistency, choose
alternative for *lamp*:
$$lamp \leftarrow \langle left, back \rangle$$

Waltz filtering:
$$S_{phone} \leftarrow \{\langle right, front \rangle, \langle right, back \rangle\}$$
$$S_{computer} \leftarrow \{\langle middle, front \rangle, \langle middle, back \rangle\}$$

Next assignment:
$$phone \leftarrow \langle right, front \rangle$$

Waltz filtering without
effect, next assignment:
$$computer \leftarrow \langle middle, back \rangle$$

Solution found:
$$lamp = \langle left, back \rangle$$
$$computer = \langle middle, back \rangle$$
$$phone = \langle right, front \rangle$$

Figure 5.5: Assignments of values to dynamic constraints performed by a backtracking algorithm combined with Waltz filtering.

the width of the ordering of the generating set is equal to the width of the generating set as such. To capture this idea more precisely, we must adapt Freuder's definitions to dynamic constraints:

Def. 15 (Width of Dynamic Constraints)
Given an ordering $\langle C_1, \ldots, C_m \rangle$ of a generating set of a dynamic network N, then the width of C_i, $i \in \{1, \ldots, m\}$, is the number of constraints in N that have C_i and a previous constraint, i.e., a constraint from $\langle C_1, \ldots, C_{i-1} \rangle$, as dependents.

Def. 16 (Width of Ordered Generating Sets)
Let $M = \langle C_1, \ldots, C_m \rangle$ be an ordered generating set of a dynamic network N, then the width of M is the maximum width of the constraints in M.

Def. 17 (Width of Generating Sets)
Let $M = \{C_1, \ldots, C_m\}$ be a generating set of a dynamic network N, then the width of M is the minimum width of all orderings of M.

A technique that aims at a minimum width ordering (but which does not guarentee to compute it) is maximum degree [Dechter and Meiri, 1989]: order the dynamic constraints of the generating set in a decreasing order of the number of constraints they depend on in the network.

An alternative to minimum width and maximum degree is the maximum cardinality heuristic [Dechter and Meiri, 1989], which may be viewed as a fixed version of dynamic search rearrangement. This heuristic selects the first constraint of the generating set arbitrarily. From then on, it appends a constraint C to the set of selected ones if C has the largest number of sisters among the constraints already selected. A dynamic constraint C is a sister of C' if there is a constraint in the network that has both C and C' as dependents. Dechter and Meiri found out that this strategy gives the best results in most cases.

Given an ordering of the constraints, the question remains how to order the values for each constraint. In cases where one wants to find a solution (as opposed to detecting inconsistency), it is a good strategy to select those values first that maximize the number of options available for future selections (cf. for example, [Dechter and Pearl, 1987] or [Haralick and Elliott, 1980]).

Another interesting heuristic that nicely combines with backtracking approaches is the min-conflict heuristic [Minton *et al.*, 1990]. The idea is to start with an initial arbitrary assignment of values to variables (which will be inconsistent in general) and to adjust the value that directly participates in conflicts, replacing it by a value that thereby generates as few conflicts as possible. The heuristic is derived from the function of a connectionist realization of a constraint network the functioning of which can be approximated by hill-climbing using the min-conflict heuristic.

5.3   Summarizing the Main Points

Since backtracking is a technique applied in many subfields of computer science, we assumed that most readers were familiar with this technique and thus kept this chapter small. In particular, we did not discuss how to implement backtracking. The interested reader will probably find examples of how to implement backtracking in most standard textbooks on computer science.

However, there are some points of **backtracking** that are special in the context of dynamic constraints, and we discussed these in this chapter. Summarizing, we can capture the following:

- In general, pure chronological backtracking is a desperate approach of a constraint satisfaction algorithm.

- Dependency-directed backtracking such as backjumping often improves the algorithm significantly.

- Look-ahead techniques and heuristics for selecting the right constraints and the right values for these constraints are means for further improvements.

Chapter 6

From Simple Filtering to Tagging

Eliminate all other factors, and the one which remains must be the truth.

—A.C. Doyle: The Sign of Four

The way we looked at constraint satisfaction algorithms in chapter 5 was from the viewpoint of backtracking, i.e., the kernel of the algorithms was some retract mechanism that was invoked when an inconsistent situation occured. We will now change our point of view, using filtering as kernel of our constraint satisfaction algorithms. This has several advantages among which the following is generally important: filtering algorithms are easy to implement on parallel hardware. We will discuss this issue in the next chapter.

However, filtering algorithms in general do not guarantee a solution of the constraint problem but result in some level of consistency such as 2-consistency in the case of AC-x, 3-consistency in the case of Allen's algorithm [Allen, 1983] and PC-x [Mackworth, 1977], and local consistency in the case of Waltz filtering. In the following, we will restrict ourselves to Waltz-like filtering, and we will use the term filtering algorithm as a shorthand for a filtering algorithm à la Waltz.

This chapter consists of two sections and a conclusion. The first section introduces and discusses a simple filtering algorithm for dynamic networks. The second one extends this algorithm by a method called tagging, which remedies the drawback of computing only local consistency instead of solutions.

6.1 A Simple Serial Filtering Algorithm

We will now have a closer look at filtering algorithms computing local consistency. In the ordinary sense, a filtering algorithm is one that successively evaluates the constraints of the network and deletes those values from the domains of the variables that are inconsistent. The algorithm of figure 6.1 and the Waltz algorithm [Waltz, 1972] are examples of filtering algorithms for ordinary constraint networks. Figure 6.2 shows a filtering algorithm for dynamic constraint networks.

Instead of just deleting incompatible values from the relations of the 0-ary dynamic constraints (which would be the direct correspondence to deleting values from the do-

Algorithm 2 (Filtering in Ordinary Constraint Networks)
Given a constraint network N.

1. *Initialize M with the set of all constraints of N.*
   (M is the set of constraints to be evaluated.)

2. **while** $M \neq \emptyset$ **do**

    (a) *Select a constraint $C \in M$, where $V_1, \ldots, V_k$ are the variables of C and $D_1, \ldots, D_k$ their respective domains.*
    *(*Domain *is used here in the sense of* variable covering.*)*

    (b) *Remove C from M.*

    (c) **for** *each V_i, where $i \in \{1, \ldots, k\}$,* **do**

        i. *Delete each value d_i from D_i for which holds:*
        the tuple $(\ldots, d_i, \ldots)$ is not an element of the relation of C.

        ii. *If D_i has been changed, then add to M all other constraints which share at least one variable with C.*

Figure 6.1: An algorithm for filtering in ordinary constraint networks.

mains of the variables in ordinary networks in step 2(c)i of algorithm 6.1), the algorithm for dynamic networks deletes values from the relations of the other dynamic constraints as well. We will call this step upward propagation (step 2(d)i). In networks with a two level structure, i.e., in networks that are translations of ordinary networks, upward propagation is not necessary: downward propagation alone is sufficient to propagate all relation changes through the network. In networks with more than two levels, however, changes of the relations are guaranteed to be considered in all parts of the network only if downward as well as upward propagation is performed. The network in figure 6.3 is an example for this: if upward propagation were missing, the restriction of *light-from* and *handedness* to $\{r\}$ would have no effect on the relation of *state*.

We will now illustrate the filtering algorithm of figure 6.2 by applying it to the network in figure 6.4. Suppose step 2a selects the *composition-table* constraint first. Then, downward propagation deletes $\succ = \{(7,5), (7,6)\}$ from the relation of c/l, since $\succ$ is incompatible with the relations of c/d and d/l. Analogously, upward propagation removes incompatible elements from the relation of *composition-table*. Now suppose c/d is selected next. Then, downward propagation leads to a reduction of the relation of *chair*, leaving the value 3 as the only element in this relation. Upward propagation has no effects in this case. After the evaluation of *composition-table* and c/d, no more constraint relations can be modified, and the algorithm terminates eventually. The result is the network shown in figure 6.5.

Filtering in ordinary networks has a number of agreeable formal properties concerning termination and uniqueness of a solution (see [Guesgen and Hertzberg, 1988]). Since every

Algorithm 3 (Filtering in Dynamic Constraint Networks)
Given a dynamic constraint network N.

1. *Initialize M with the constraints of arity greater than zero.*

2. **while** $M \neq \emptyset$ **do**

    (a) *Select a constraint $C \in M$, where $\delta(C) = \{C_1, \ldots, C_k\}$ and $R, R_1, \ldots, R_k$ are the relations of $C, C_1, \ldots, C_k$, respectively.*

    (b) *Remove C from M, i.e., $M \leftarrow M \setminus \{C\}$*

    (c) (Downward Propagation)

    for *each C_i, where $i \in \{1, \ldots, k\}$,* **do**

        i. Delete the values d_i from R_i that cannot be completed to a tuple $(\ldots, d_i, \ldots) \in R$.

        ii. **if** *R_i has been changed,* **then** *add to M all other constraints that C_i depends on, i.e., $M \leftarrow M \cup \{C' \mid C_i \in \delta(C')\} \setminus \{C\}$*

    (d) (Upward Propagation)

    for C **do**

        i. Delete the values d from R if $d \notin R_1 \times \cdots \times R_k$

        ii. **if** *R has been changed,* **then** *add to M the constraints that C depends on, i.e., $M \leftarrow M \cup \{C' \mid C \in \delta(C')\}$*

Figure 6.2: An algorithm for filtering in dynamic constraint networks.

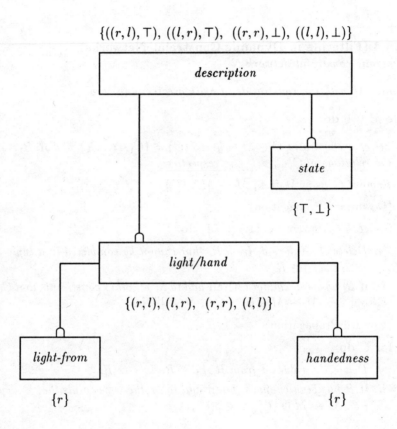

Figure 6.3: A derivative of the lighting network in figure 3.9, in which the value l has been deleted from the relations of *light-from* and *handedness*.

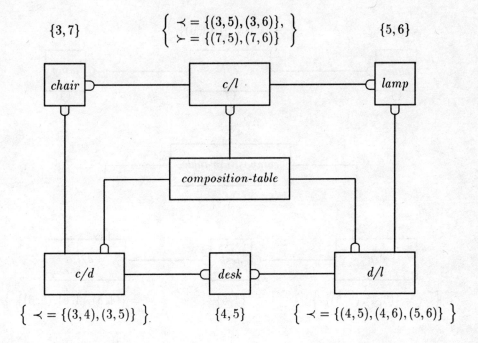

Figure 6.4: A dynamic constraint network for the office scenario of figure 2.1. The network is identical with the one in figure 3.6.

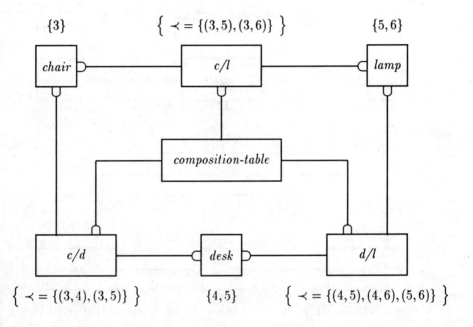

Figure 6.5: Locally consistent dynamic constraint network obtained by applying the filtering algorithm to the network of figure 6.4.

dynamic network has a corresponding ordinary network (cf. definition 7), we can directly apply these results to dynamic networks:

Prop. 12 (Properties of Filtering)
The following holds for the algorithm of figure 6.2:

1. *The filtering algorithm terminates if the domains are finite, independently of the ordering in which the constraints are selected in step 2a.*

2. *It is semi-decidable whether the algorithm terminates if the domains are infinite.* **In** *this context, semi-decidability means: if there is at least one ordering of constraints in step 2a that results in the termination of the algorithm, then any ordering will do as long as it is fair, i.e., each constraint is evaluated at least once* **and after its** *variables have been changed.*

3. *If all domains are finite or the selection order is fair, then the result—if one exists— is unique.*

4. *The result of the algorithm is local consistency as defined in definition 14.*

The above shows that filtering algorithms for ordinary constraint networks can be easily adapted to dynamic networks. However, like in the case of ordinary networks, they compute only local consistency and not necessarily a solution of a given dynCSP. In the next section, we will introduce a tagging algorithm to overcome this drawback.

6.2   Filtering with Tagging

6.2.1   The Principle of Tagging

Consider, for example, the above desk problem in a slightly modified version. This time, we are only interested in the relative positions of the utensils with respect to the y-axis, i.e., each of the dynamic constraints *lamp*, *computer*, and *phone* has the domain $\{front, back\}$. Let us assume that, for some weird reasons, two utensils must not be placed in the same row, which leads us to the dynamic network shown in figure 6.6. A filtering algorithm applied to this network would have no effects, since, independently of which constraint is evaluated, none of the values is removed from the relations of the constraints. On the other hand, none of them contributes to a solution of the problem (the problem is inconsistent), and thus all of them should be deleted. To overcome this drawback, we extend the filtering algorithm by what is called tagging. The idea of tagging is to maintain global relationships among the values during the filtering process.

So the question is: how can global relationships among values be represented in such a way that they can be handled efficiently during filtering? One answer is to construct higher-order constraints until an m-ary constraint (m denoting the number of 0-ary constraints in the network) is obtained that represents the relation of the network [Freuder, 1978]. The solution presented here is to tag values during the filtering process, assigning identical tags to values whose combination satisfies the constraints.

In particular, this means that an additional step is performed which assigns tags to the values that are admissible with respect to a constraint. Suppose that the l/c constraint

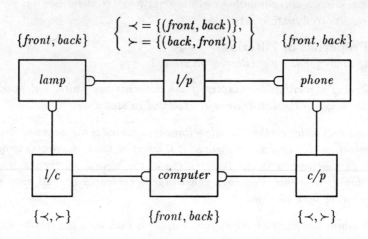

Figure 6.6: Another constraint network for the desk example.

is selected for evaluation, then the algorithm computes the following sets of tagged values as new relations for *lamp* and *computer*, respectively:

$$R_{lamp} \quad = \quad \{front_i, back_j\}$$
$$R_{computer} \quad = \quad \{front_j, back_i\}$$

The indices i and j denote two different tags, meaning that if *front* is chosen as the value of *lamp*, then *back* must be the value of *computer*, and vice versa.

On the basis of these relations, another constraint, let us say *c/p*, can be evaluated. Now we have the case that the values of one of *c/p*'s dependents, *computer*, are tagged but those of the other dependent, *phone*, are not. The tagging algorithm handles this case by passing on tags from *computer* to *phone*, resulting in the following relations:

$$R_{lamp} \quad = \quad \{front_i, back_j\}$$
$$R_{computer} \quad = \quad \{front_j, back_i\}$$
$$R_{phone} \quad = \quad \{front_i, back_j\}$$

When the constraint on *lamp* and *phone*, *l/p*, is evaluated, the inconsistency can be detected (as opposed to the pure filtering algorithm), as the values of both *lamp* and *phone* are tagged. In particular, the algorithm performs the following three steps:

1. $(front_i, back_j)$ and $(back_j, front_i)$ would be permitted value combinations with respect to the relation of *l/p*.

2. $(front_i, front_i)$ and $(back_j, back_j)$ would be permitted value combinations with respect to the tags.

3. The intersection of the value combinations computed in steps 1 and 2 is empty, which means inconsistency.

The tagging technique presented so far is not yet correct for all types of constraint networks. For example, if tags are assigned in different parts of a network, they are distinct, and thus the corresponding values are considered inconsistent, although this need not be the case. Especially when we consider parallel implementations of the tagging algorithm (as we will do in chapter 7), this is of interest. Beyond that, hierarchical networks, i.e., networks with constraints which have dependents which have dependents themselves and so on, cannot be handled adequately. These shortcomings can be overcome by using structured tags, which we will introduce in the next section.

6.2.2 Structured Tags and their Evaluation

The tags that are propagated among the constraints of a dynamic network are tuples, each component of such a tuple being associated with a constraint of the network. Suppose that the network consists of m constraints with arity greater than zero, and that there is an ordering on these constraints. Then, every tag is an m-tuple where the ith value in the tuple is the tag assigned by the ith constraint. For example, assuming the ordering $l/c < c/p < l/p$, the value $front_{(2,1,3)}$ means that l/c, c/p, and l/p assigned the tags 2, 1, and 3, respectively. The advantage of using tuples as tags is obvious: each subtag in the tuple can be uniquely mapped to a constraint of the network which facilitates their handling.

From a more global perspective, tagging may be viewed as filtering operating on a more complex domain. Instead of a domain D, the extended domain $D_i \times I_1 \times \cdots \times I_m$ is used, where I_j is the set of tags that may be assigned by C_j and n the number of constraints of the network. This perspective may be helpful from time to time. Be aware, however, that it does not capture all aspects of tagging. In particular, it does not respect the idea of tags being generated dynamically.

Before a constraint C is evaluated, the tags occurring in the relation of C and the relations of C's dependents are simplified. Suppose that the ith constraint of the network is to be evaluated, then only the ith position in the tag is of interest. Hence, each tag is replaced with its ith component. For example, the value $front_{(2,1,3)}$ is simplified to $front_1$ when c/p is to be evaluated. The projection assures that a constraint can only manipulate the part of the tag which is related to the constraint.

Besides pure filtering, the evaluation of a constraint C with dependents $C_1, \ldots, C_k$ means not just checking whether $d = (d_1, \ldots, d_k)$ is consistent with the relation R_C of C and d_i with R_{C_i} but also matching the simplified tags associated with $d, d_1, \ldots, d_k$. This is done in the following way. First, the common tag of $d, d_1, \ldots, d_k$ is computed, which is a new tag if all values are untagged. If some values are already provided with tags, and if all of them are identical, then the common tag is determined by this tag; otherwise it is undefined. For example, the common tag of $(front, back)_-$, $front_2$, and $back_-$ is 2, whereas the common tag of $(front, back)_-$, $front_2$, and $back_3$ is undefined. If the common tag of $d, d_1, \ldots, d_k$ is undefined, the tuple represents an invalid value combination with respect to the tags, and therefore $d, d_1, \ldots, d_k$ are deleted from the respective relations. In the other case, the tags of the values in the tuple are updated by the common tag.

After the evaluation of a constraint, the projection procedure which has simplified the tags must be reversed. For that purpose, the subtags, i.e., the tags resulting from the evaluation process, are merged with the original tags. After that, tags that have been merged with the same subtag are unified. Unification in this context means: the components of the tags are compared; if common tags exist for all components, then the common tags are substituted for the components; otherwise, unification is not possible and the corresponding values are deleted.

For example, assuming that $front_{(1,-,-)}$ is a value in $R_{computer}$ and $back_{(-,-,3)}$ a value in R_{phone} and that the second constraint of network, c/p, is to be evaluated, the tags are manipulated as follows:

$$
\begin{array}{lll}
\text{Simplifying:} & R_{computer} & \ni\ front_{-} \\
& R_{phone} & \ni\ back_{-} \\[2mm]
\text{Evaluating:} & R_{computer} & \ni\ front_{2} \\
& R_{phone} & \ni\ back_{2} \\[2mm]
\text{Merging:} & R_{computer} & \ni\ front_{(1,2,-)} \\
& R_{phone} & \ni\ back_{(-,2,3)} \\[2mm]
\text{Unifying:} & R_{computer} & \ni\ front_{(1,2,3)} \\
& R_{phone} & \ni\ back_{(1,2,3)}
\end{array}
$$

6.2.3　An Example

We will now apply the tagging algorithm to the network of figure 6.6. The initial relations of the dynamic constraints in this network are:

$$
\begin{array}{llllll}
R_{lamp} &=& R_{computer} &=& R_{phone} &=& \{front_{(-,-,-)}, back_{(-,-,-)}\} \\
R_{l/c} &=& R_{c/p} &=& R_{l/p} &=& \{(front, back)_{(-,-,-)}, (back, front)_{(-,-,-)}\}
\end{array}
$$

Let us assume that the algorithm chooses l/c to be the first constraint in the evaluation sequence, then tags are provided for $lamp$, $computer$, and l/c:

$$
\begin{array}{lll}
\text{Simplifying:} & R_{lamp} &= \{front_{-}, back_{-}\} \\
& R_{computer} &= \{front_{-}, back_{-}\} \\
& R_{l/c} &= \{(front, back)_{-}, (back, front)_{-}\} \\[2mm]
\text{Evaluating:} & R_{lamp} &= \{front_{1}, back_{2}\} \\
& R_{computer} &= \{front_{2}, back_{1}\} \\
& R_{l/c} &= \{(front, back)_{1}, (back, front)_{2}\} \\[2mm]
\text{Merging:} & R_{lamp} &= \{front_{(1,-,-)}, back_{(2,-,-)}\} \\
& R_{computer} &= \{front_{(2,-,-)}, back_{(1,-,-)}\} \\
& R_{l/c} &= \{(front, back)_{(1,-,-)}, (back, front)_{(2,-,-)}\} \\[2mm]
\text{Unifying:} & R_{lamp} &= \{front_{(1,-,-)}, back_{(2,-,-)}\} \\
& R_{computer} &= \{front_{(2,-,-)}, back_{(1,-,-)}\} \\
& R_{l/c} &= \{(front, back)_{(1,-,-)}, (back, front)_{(2,-,-)}\}
\end{array}
$$

Now either c/p or l/p may be evaluated. Let us suppose that c/p is the one selected to be evaluated next. Then the tags of *computer* (*phone* does not yet have any tags) are simplified, replacing each tag tuple with its second component (which is in accordance to the ordering $l/c < c/p < l/p$). None of the resulting values do have tags, so new tags are provided which are unified with the former tags of *computer*:

Simplifying:	$R_{computer}$	$=$	$\{front_-, back_-\}$
	R_{phone}	$=$	$\{front_-, back_-\}$
	$R_{c/p}$	$=$	$\{(front, back)_-, (back, front)_-\}$

Evaluating:	$R_{computer}$	$=$	$\{front_3, back_4\}$
	R_{phone}	$=$	$\{front_4, back_3\}$
	$R_{c/p}$	$=$	$\{(front, back)_3, (back, front)_4\}$

Merging:	$R_{computer}$	$=$	$\{front_{(2,3,-)}, back_{(1,4,-)}\}$
	R_{phone}	$=$	$\{front_{(-,4,-)}, back_{(-,3,-)}\}$
	$R_{c/p}$	$=$	$\{(front, back)_{(-,3,-)}, (back, front)_{(-,4,-)}\}$

Unifying:	$R_{computer}$	$=$	$\{front_{(2,3,-)}, back_{(1,4,-)}\}$
	R_{phone}	$=$	$\{front_{(1,4,-)}, back_{(2,3,-)}\}$
	$R_{c/p}$	$=$	$\{(front, back)_{(2,3,-)}, (back, front)_{(1,4,-)}\}$

With that, the current relations look as follows:

$$
\begin{aligned}
R_{lamp} &= \{front_{(1,-,-)}, back_{(2,-,-)}\} \\
R_{computer} &= \{front_{(2,3,-)}, back_{(1,4,-)}\} \\
R_{phone} &= \{front_{(1,4,-)}, back_{(2,3,-)}\} \\
R_{l/c} &= \{(front, back)_{(1,-,-)}, (back, front)_{(2,-,-)}\} \\
R_{c/p} &= \{(front, back)_{(2,3,-)}, (back, front)_{(1,4,-)}\} \\
R_{l/p} &= \{(front, back)_{(-,-,-)}, (back, front)_{(-,-,-)}\}
\end{aligned}
$$

When now the constraint between *lamp* and *phone*, l/p, is evaluated, the tagging algorithm assignes the empty set as relation to *lamp*, *phone*, and l/p, since the tags cannot be unified:

Simplifying:	R_{lamp}	$=$	$\{front_-, back_-\}$
	R_{phone}	$=$	$\{front_-, back_-\}$
	$R_{l/p}$	$=$	$\{(front, back)_-, (back, front)_-\}$

Evaluating:	R_{lamp}	$=$	$\{front_5, back_6\}$
	R_{phone}	$=$	$\{front_6, back_5\}$
	$R_{l/p}$	$=$	$\{(front, back)_5, (back, front)_6\}$

Merging:	R_{lamp}	$=$	$\{front_{(1,-,5)}, back_{(2,-,6)}\}$
	R_{phone}	$=$	$\{front_{(1,4,6)}, back_{(2,3,5)}\}$
	$R_{l/p}$	$=$	$\{(front, back)_{(-,-,5)}, (back, front)_{(-,-,6)}\}$

Unifying:	R_{lamp}	$=$	$\emptyset$
	R_{phone}	$=$	$\emptyset$
	$R_{l/p}$	$=$	$\emptyset$

We could stop the tagging algorithm at this point, since a totally connected constraint network is inconsistent if and only if at least one relation becomes empty during tagging. However, for reasons of completeness, we will show how the information that the network is inconsistenct is propagated to every constraint in the network. For this purpose, l/c is evaluated again:

Simplifying:	R_{lamp}	$=$	$\emptyset$
	$R_{computer}$	$=$	$\{front_2, back_1\}$
	$R_{l/c}$	$=$	$\{(front, back)_1, (back, front)_2\}$

Evaluating:	R_{lamp}	$=$	$\emptyset$
	$R_{computer}$	$=$	$\emptyset$
	$R_{l/c}$	$=$	$\emptyset$

Merging:	R_{lamp}	$=$	$\emptyset$
	$R_{computer}$	$=$	$\emptyset$
	$R_{l/c}$	$=$	$\emptyset$

Unifying:	R_{lamp}	$=$	$\emptyset$
	$R_{computer}$	$=$	$\emptyset$
	$R_{l/c}$	$=$	$\emptyset$

And finally, the algorithm evaluates c/p for the second time, restricting the remaining relations to the empty set:

Simplifying:	$R_{computer}$	$=$	$\emptyset$
	R_{phone}	$=$	$\emptyset$
	$R_{c/p}$	$=$	$\{(front, back)_3, (back, front)_4\}$

Evaluating:	$R_{computer}$	$=$	$\emptyset$
	R_{phone}	$=$	$\emptyset$
	$R_{c/p}$	$=$	$\emptyset$

Merging:	$R_{computer}$	$=$	$\emptyset$
	R_{phone}	$=$	$\emptyset$
	$R_{c/p}$	$=$	$\emptyset$

Unifying:	$R_{computer}$	$=$	$\emptyset$
	R_{phone}	$=$	$\emptyset$
	$R_{c/p}$	$=$	$\emptyset$

In general, not all values are removed from the relations of the constraints. The remaining values specify the solution(s) of the dynamic constraint network. In particular, this means that it is admissible to combine those values to solution tuples that have the same tag. We will illustrate this by modifying the desk example in the following way:

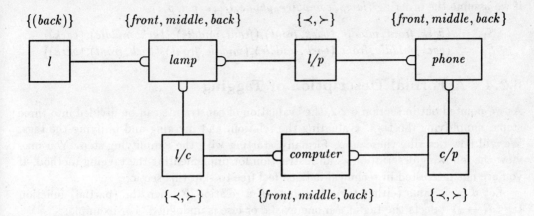

Figure 6.7: The third constraint network for the desk example.

1. Until now, the top of our desk consisted of two rows, *front* and *back*. We add an additional row, *middle*, to these two rows and extend the constraint relations accordingly:

$$R_{lamp} = R_{computer} = R_{phone} = \{front, middle, back\}$$
$$R_{l/c} = R_{c/p} = R_{l/p} = \{(front, middle), (front, back),$$
$$(middle, front), (middle, back),$$
$$(back, front), (back, middle)\}$$

2. We insert a unary constraint l with relation $\{(back)\}$ into the network which has *lamp* as dependent (cf. figure 6.7), stating that the lamp must be placed somewhere in the back row of the desk.

The network of figure 6.7 consists of four constraints that have an arity greater than zero. Thus, the algorithm assigns 4-ary tags, the fourth component corresponding to the constraint l and the other components corresponding to l/c, c/p, and l/p as in the example above. Assuming that l is evaluated first, followed by an evaluation of l/c, c/p, and l/p as in the example above, the algorithm results in the following relations:

$$R_{lamp} = \{back_{(2,4,6,1)}, back_{(3,5,7,1)}\}$$
$$R_{computer} = \{front_{(2,4,6,1)}, middle_{(3,5,7,1)}\}$$
$$R_{phone} = \{middle_{(2,4,6,1)}, front_{(3,5,7,1)}\}$$
$$R_{l/c} = \{(back, front)_{(2,4,6,1)}, (back, middle)_{(3,5,7,1)}\}$$
$$R_{c/p} = \{(front, middle)_{(2,4,6,1)}, (middle, front)_{(3,5,7,1)}\}$$
$$R_{l/p} = \{(back, middle)_{(2,4,6,1)}, (back, front)_{(3,5,7,1)}\}$$
$$R_{l} = \{(back)_{(2,4,6,1)}, (back)_{(3,5,7,1)}\}$$

The relations represent the two solutions of the constraint network, which look as follows if we assume the ordering $(lamp, computer, phone, l/c, c/p, l/p, l)$:

$$S_1 = (back, front, middle, (back, front), (front, middle), (back, middle), (back))$$
$$S_2 = (back, middle, front, (back, middle), (middle, front), (back, front), (back))$$

6.2.4   A Formal Description of Tagging

As we pointed out in section 6.2.2, the evaluation of constraints can be divided into three steps: simplifying the tags, evaluating the relation, and merging and unifying the tags. We will now describe these steps formally, starting with the simplifying step. You may view the following description as an instruction for implementing the tagging method. If you are not interested in technical details, feel free to skip this section.

Let d be a value (either tagged or not) of a relation R, then the (partial) function $\text{tag} : R \to I\!N$ selects the tag of d if one exists, or else is undefined. For example:

$$\text{tag}(front_5) = 5$$
$$\text{tag}(back_-) = \text{undefined}$$

If the tag of d is a tuple, one may be interested only in a certain component of the tuple. The function $\text{tag}_j : R \to I\!N$ selects the jth component of d's tag. For example:

$$\text{tag}_2(front_{(-,5,-)}) = 5$$
$$\text{tag}_3(front_{(-,5,-)}) = \text{undefined}$$

Analogously, $\text{val} : R \to R$ is a function that removes the tag from a value d. For example:

$$\text{val}(front_5) = front$$
$$\text{val}(back_-) = back$$

Suppose that C is the ιth constraint of the network. When C is to be evaluated, only the ιth components of the tags are of interest. Hence, every (tagged) value d that belongs to the relation R of a dependent of C is simplified to a value d^s before C is evaluated, applying the following scheme:

$$d^s = \text{tagval}(\text{val}(d), \text{tag}_\iota(d))$$

The function $\text{tagval} : R \times I\!N \to R$ composes an untagged value and an integer to a tagged value, i.e., tagval has the following property:

$$d = \text{tagval}(\text{val}(d), \text{tag}(d))$$

The projection on the ιth component of each tag assures that C can only manipulate that part of a tag which is related to the constraint.

We will now describe how a k-ary constraint C is applied to simplified values. The description uses the following conventions:

- Let d^s be a tagged value that results from d by applying the above simplification scheme, then d is called a source of d^s.[1]

---

[1] A value may have more than one source.

- The expression $\mathrm{tag}(d_i^s) \doteq t$ means that if $\mathrm{tag}(d_i^s)$ is defined then it is equal to t.

- The function ctag determines the common tag of a tuple of values, i.e.:

$$
\mathrm{ctag}(d_1^s,\ldots,d_k^s) = \begin{cases} \text{new tag,} & \text{if } \forall i \in \{1,\ldots,k\} : \\ & \quad \mathrm{tag}(d_i^s) \text{ is undefined} \\ \\ t, & \text{if } \exists i \in \{1,\ldots,k\} : \\ & \quad \mathrm{tag}(d_i^s) \text{ is defined} \\ & \text{and } \forall i \in \{1,\ldots,k\} : \\ & \quad \mathrm{tag}(d_i^s) \doteq t \\ \\ \text{undefined,} & \text{else} \end{cases}
$$

With that, the evaluation of a k-ary constraint C with respect to tags is straightforward. In addition to the delete operations performed in a standard filtering algorithm (compare the steps 2(c)i and 2(d)i of the algorithm in figure 6.2), the tags in each tuple $(d_1,\ldots,d_k)$ that is considered for deletion must be matched with each other. In particular, the following steps are performed:

1. A tuple $(d_1^s,\ldots,d_k^s)$ is deleted, if its values do not have a common tag, i.e., if $\mathrm{ctag}(d_1^s,\ldots,d_k^s)$ is undefined:[2]

2. If $\mathrm{ctag}(d_1^s,\ldots,d_k^s)$ is defined and if $(d_1^s,\ldots,d_k^s)$ is an element of the relation of C, the tags in $(d_1^s,\ldots,d_k^s)$ are replaced with $\mathrm{ctag}(d_1^s,\ldots,d_k^s)$.

After the evaluation of a constraint, the values that have been changed must be merged and unified. To formalize this step, we define a function ctag*, which is the extension of *ctag* to tuples (m denotes the number of constraints with arity greater than zero):

$$
\mathrm{ctag}^*(d_1^u,\ldots,d_k^u) = \begin{cases} (t_1,\ldots,t_m), & \text{if } \forall i \in \{1,\ldots,k\}\forall j \in \{1,\ldots,m\} : \\ & \quad \mathrm{tag}_j(d_i^u) \doteq t_j \\ \\ \text{undefined,} & \text{else} \end{cases}
$$

On the basis of this definition, the merging procedure can be denoted as follows. Let C be again the ιth constraint of the network (the arity of C being k), let $(d_1^s,\ldots,d_k^s)$ be a tuple resulting from the evaluation of C, and let d_i, $i \in \{1,\ldots,k\}$, be a source of d_i^s, then:

1. Replace the ιth components of the tags in $(d_1,\ldots,d_k)$ by $\mathrm{ctag}(d_1^s,\ldots,d_k^s)$, and let $(d_1^u,\ldots,d_k^u)$ be the resulting tuple.

2. If $\mathrm{ctag}^*(d_1^u,\ldots,d_k^u)$ is undefined, then delete $(d_1^u,\ldots,d_k^u)$ from the relation of C and the d_j, $j \in \{1,\ldots,k\}$, from the relations of C's dependents; else substitute $\mathrm{ctag}^*(d_1^u,\ldots,d_k^u)$ for the tags of $(d_1^u,\ldots,d_k^u)$.

---

[2] $\mathrm{ctag}(d_1^s,\ldots,d_k^s)$ is undefined, iff there are at least two tags that are not compatible, i.e., $\exists i,j \in \{1,\ldots,k\}$ such that $\mathrm{tag}(d_i^s)$ and $\mathrm{tag}(d_j^s)$ are defined but $\mathrm{tag}(d_i^s) \neq \mathrm{tag}(d_j^s)$.

6.3   Conclusion

In the previous sections, we discussed filtering algorithms for dynamic constraint networks. We started with a simple filtering algorithm for computing local consistency and introduced an extension of filtering to use it as a general constraint satisfaction algorithm. In contrast to a backtracking approach, filtering combined with tagging is a kind of breadth-first method for solving dynCSPs. Although it is more expensive to compute all solutions instead of looking for one tuple that satisfies the constraints, this makes sense, as many dynCSPs have a huge search space but only a few solutions.

When developing the tagging algorithm we did not hope to find a polynomial algorithm for NP-complete problems, and so our approach is exponential in the worst case. As the constraint network of figure 6.7 suggests, the combinatorial explosion occurs when values are duplicated excessively. Let m be the number of 0-ary constraint in the dynamic network and l be the maximal number of values occurring in the relations of the constraints. Then—in the worst case—the number of tagged values is l^m, which leads to the exponential worst-case behavior of filtering with tagging.

However, an advantage of filtering with tagging is that a parallel version can be implemented easily. We will discuss this topic in the following chapter, starting with a parallel implementation that assumes only a limited number of processors and ending with a massively parallel one.

Chapter 7

Appoaches to Filtering in Parallel

Filtering algorithms are easy to implement on multiprocessors (cf., for example, Kasif [1989], Rosenfeld [1975], and Samal & Henderson [1987]). Moreover, there are also massively parallel filtering algorithms: AC Chip which can be implemented directly in VLSI, and ACP which has been designed for SIMD computers like the Connection Machine (see [Cooper and Swain, 1988] as reference for both algorithms). They are closely related to Mohr and Henderson's AC-4 algorithm [Mohr and Henderson, 1986], which is optimal for computing 2-consistency on single-processor machines.

This chapter shows how filtering can be performed in parallel. We will start with a simple parallel filtering algorithm. Then, we will discuss how the tagging method may be incorporated into the algorithm. Last but not least, we will describe a massively parallel filtering approach using connectionist networks.

7.1   A Simple Parallel Filtering Algorithm

There is a variety of parallel versions of filtering algorithms, all of which we do not want to discuss here. Instead we will introduce a simple parallel implementation of filtering. To make the introduction easier, we assume for a moment that the number of processors is greater than or equal to the number of dynamic constraints in the given network. With this assumption, the skeleton of a parallel filtering algorithm may look like that shown in figure 7.1. The idea of the algorithm is to associate a processor with each dynamic constraint of the network, and to allow communication between processors that correspond to adjacent constraints.

Even though it is not the purpose of this section to give an elaborate description of how to implement the algorithm, a short discussion of a potential conflict seems appropriate. Suppose, two dynamic constraints C_1 and C_2 have a dependent C in common, i.e., $C \in \delta(C_1) \cap \delta(C_2)$. Now assume, C_1 and C_2 receive the current relation from C concurrently, but C_2 sends its result back to C before C_1 does. The question is: Do we get a correct result although C_1 has been evaluated with obsolete information? The answer to this

Algorithm 4 (Skeleton of a Parallel Filtering Algorithm)
Given a dynamic constraint network N.

1. *Assign a processor to each dynamic constraint of N.*

2. *Install communication links in accordance with the dependency structure in N, i.e., communication is allowed only between a constraint and its dependents.*

3. *Activate the processors: a constraint receives the current relations of its dependents, deletes those elements from the relations (including its own relation) that are incompatible, and sends back the result to its dependents which intersect the incoming relations.*

4. *Stop the processors and return the current constraint relations when no further relation changes are made.*

Figure 7.1: Skeleton of a simple parallel filtering algorithm.

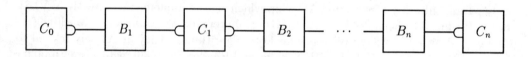

Figure 7.2: A dynamic constraint network with a chain structure.

question is that an additional evaluation of C_2 would lead to the same result as the one we would obtain if C_1 and C_2 were evaluated sequentially. The proof of this (see [Guesgen and Hertzberg, 1988]) is based on the following:

- The relation of C is a subset of the one that would result if C_1 were evaluated but C_2 is not.

- The relation of C is a superset of the one that would result if C_2 were evaluated after C_1.

In the worst case, the algorithm does not have a real parallel behavior. Consider, for example, figure 7.2 which shows a chain of alternating 0-ary constraints $C_0, \ldots, C_n$ and binary constraints $B_1, \ldots, B_n$ with the following relations:

$$
\begin{aligned}
C_0 &= \{front\} \\
C_1 = \cdots = C_n &= \{front, back\} \\
B_1 = \cdots = B_n &= \{(front, front), (back, back)\}
\end{aligned}
$$

The parallel algorithm of figure 7.1 shows the same behavior as the corresponding serial one in this example, since the value *front* of C_0 must be propagated through the chain, which can only be done sequentially.

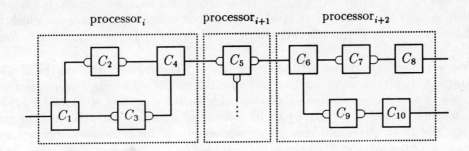

Figure 7.3: Parallel implementation with a limited number of processors.

In the case where the number of available processors may be lower than the number of constraints in the dynamic network, the scheme can be extended as follows. Let p be the number of available processors and n be the number of constraints in the dynamic network. If $p \geq n$, then each dynamic constraint can be associated with its own processor. If $p < n$, then some processors obtain subnetworks, performing serial filtering on these (cf. figure 7.3).

7.2   Parallel Filtering with Tagging

In principle, the tagging algorithm works like a common filtering algorithm. The difference is in the values that are propagated. In the case of tagging, they contain more information than just possible values of the constraint relations, namely their relationships to other values. To be more precise: filtering with tagging may be viewed as simple filtering on the extended domain $D_i \times I_1 \times \cdots \times I_n$, where D_i is the original domain of the dynamic constraint C_i, I_j the set of tags that may be assigned by C_j, and n the number of constraints of the network. Applying the algorithm of figure 7.1 to the extended domain results in a parallel realization of tagging.

However, the approach of filtering the extended domain $D_i \times I_1 \times \cdots \times I_n$ is an idealized and unrealistic version of what tagging actually does, since in reality, we cannot expect all elements of such a huge domain to be given. Rather, it is necessary to apply some instantiation mechanism which generates new elements when they are required. In the algorithm of section 6.2, the instantiation mechanism is tagging itself: during the evaluation of a constraint, values like $front_-$, for example, are transformed into values like $front_2$ and $front_5$.

Tagging must be guaranteed to be monotonic, i.e., a more general value (for example, $front_{(2,-,-)}$) may be replaced only with a more specific one (for example, $front_{(2,3,-)}$) and never the other way round. In the serial case, one gets this guarantee for free, since a constraint is always evaluated with respect to the most recent values, which are replaced during evaluation by more specific ones, which in turn are used by another constraint, and so on. When filtering is performed in parallel, monotonicity may be violated when the read/write operations of two constraints with common variables overlap. In this case, a good strategy is to perform updates only on those constraint relations for which the updates are monotonic. An elaborate description of correct update strategies can be found in [Ho *et al.*, 1991].

We will finish this section with some remarks on the complexity of the parallel filtering/tagging algorithm. As pointed out in section 6.2, the serial filtering/tagging algorithm is exponential in the worst case. The same holds for the algorithm of figure 7.1 applied with tagging. However, there are parallel filtering algorithms with sublinear time complexity, and these algorithms may be considered as well for being used together with tagging. An example of such an algorithm, intended for computing arc consistency in binary constraint networks, is introduced in [Cooper and Swain, 1988, appendix D]. Since the algorithm described there is logarithmic in the number of values, it compensates for the possibly exponential number of tagged values. The tradeoff, however, is that the algorithm requires an exponential number of processors.

The worst case behavior of the algorithm, however, is only one aspect to be considered. Even more important is how the performance of the parallel algorithm is compared with the performance of the serial one. To test the performance, both algorithms have been implemented in the constraint satisfaction system CONSAT [Guesgen, 1989a; Ho *et al.*, 1991] and have been applied to a standard problem of a kind of basic spatial reasoning well-known from the literature: a constraint network which assigns three-dimensional edge labelings to line drawings in a polyhedral world [Horn, 1986, page 358]. The result is summarized in the following table, which lists the factors (in dependence on the number of processors used) by which parallel tagging is faster than the serial one (see [Ho *et al.*, 1991] for details):

Processors	2	3	4	5	6
Speedup	2.1	3.0	3.9	4.5	5.0

7.3 Massively Parallel Filtering

In the previous sections, we introduced filtering and the extension of filtering by tagging. We described how filtering and filtering with tagging could be realized on one-processor machines, and sketched a parallel implementation for multiprocessors. Continuing our effort of parallelizing filtering, we will now discuss a connectionist approach of filtering based on the work described in [Cooper and Swain, 1988].

This section is organized as follows: we will first give a short introduction to connectionist systems and the part of [Cooper and Swain, 1988] that is essential for our approach. We will then show how Cooper and Swain's approach can be extended to a complete constraint satisfaction algorithm, using Gödel numbers to represent possible paths of solutions. The approach is closely related to the tagging method described in the previous sections.

7.3.1 Connectionist Representation

Connectionist systems aim at modeling aspects of the human brain on an abstract computational level (cf. [Feldman and Ballard, 1982]). A motivation for using this metaphor lies in the following observation: In traditional AI, cognitive tasks are modeled as inferences performed on symbolic structures, being intractable with respect to the time they require; on the other hand, human beings can deal with a wide range of these tasks in real-time, i.e., they can handle many cognitive tasks with extreme efficiency. To underscore this efficiency, Shastri [1989] labeled such inferences *reflexive* (in contrast to the *reflective* inferences performed in a traditional AI system).[1]

To obtain a system that is able to perform reflexive rather than reflective inferences, Shastri suggested a list of characteristics:

- The system must be massively parallel, i.e., it must use a huge amount of processors.

- It must operate without a central controller.

- It must use a high degree of connectivity, realized by hard-wired links.

- It must not use complex messages but simple ones, for example, scalars.

These characteristics lead us to the metaphor of connectionist reasoning: assign a processing element to each unit of information, express dependencies between them by links, and pass messages through the net by spreading activations.

The connectionist networks discussed in [Cooper and Swain, 1988] are in accordance with these characteristics: a separate node is dedicated to each relation element of each constraint of the dynamic network. This approach is in analogy to de Kleer's way of representing constraint networks as propositional-clauses [de Kleer, 1989].

In the major part of this text, we used arbitrary k-ary dynamic constraints which we put together to arbitrary complex networks. We will now restrict ourselves to simple dynamic constraint networks to keep the rest of this section easy to read. In particular, we will make the following restrictions:[2]

1. All dynamic constraints of the network are either binary constraints, i.e., constraints with two dependents, or 0-ary constraints, i.e., constraints without dependents.

2. All dependents of a binary constraint are of arity 0.

Suppose N is a dynamic constraint network fulfilling the above restrictions. Then, N can be divided into two disjoint subsets N_0 and N_2, where N_0 contains all 0-ary constraints and N_2 all binary constraints. Each binary constraint can uniquely be denoted by the pair of its dependents, i.e., if a constraint has dependents C_1 and C_2, it can be denoted as $\langle C_1, C_2 \rangle$. Furthermore, we can assume that the network be complete, i.e., every pair of 0-ary constraints is connected by a binary constraint.

Let D_0 be the union of the domains of the constraints in N_0, and $D_2 = D_0 \times D_0$ the union of those in N_2. We represent each element of each 0-ary constraint by a connectionist

---

[1] Note that Shastri uses the term *reflective* in a different sense than we do in chapter 3.

[2] The restrictions lead us to dynamic networks that directly correspond to ordinary binary constraint networks, consisting of variables and binary constraints.

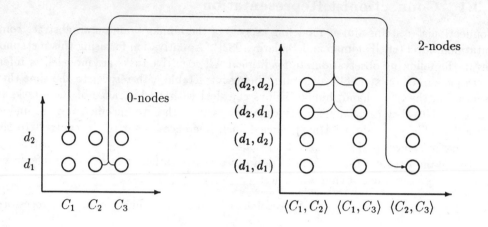

Figure 7.4: Scheme of a connectionist network for constraint satisfaction. The network has two different types of links: each 2-node is linked with the corresponding pair of 0-nodes and each 0-node is linked with the corresponding quadruple of 2-nodes. Note that not all links are depicted.

node and denote this node by $\langle C, d \rangle$, where $C \in N_0$ and $d \in D_0$. Furthermore, we introduce a connectionist node for each element of each binary constraint and denote this node by $\langle C_1, C_2, d_1, d_2 \rangle$, where $\langle C_1, C_2 \rangle \in N_2$ and $(d_1, d_2) \in D_2$. Because of symmetry, $\langle C_1, C_2, d_1, d_2 \rangle$ and $\langle C_2, C_1, d_2, d_1 \rangle$ denote the same node.

This representation corresponds to the one in [Cooper and Swain, 1988]. As it is shown there, 0-nodes and 2-nodes can be connected in such a way that the resulting network computes an 2-consistent solution for the corresponding constraint satisfaction problem (cf. figure 7.4). For that purpose, the nodes are initialized as follows:

- A 0-node $\langle C, d \rangle$ obtains potential 1, if d is an element of the relation of C; else it obtains potential 0.

- A 2-node $\langle C_1, C_2, d_1, d_2 \rangle$ obtains potential 1, if (d_1, d_2) is an element of the relation of $\langle C_1, C_2 \rangle$; else it obtains potential 0.

For convenience, we will use $\langle C, d \rangle$, for example, for both: either for referring to the potential of a node or for denoting the node itself.

In analogy to the delete operations of the filtering algorithms in chapter 6, a 0-node is reset to 0 if one cannot find at least one 0-node for every other 0-ary constraint such that the binary constraint between this 0-node and the given 0-node is satisfied (in other words: the corresponding 2-node must have potential 1). This rule is called the arc consistency label discarding rule [Hummel and Zucker, 1983]:

> Discard value (label) d at the 0-ary constraint C if $\exists C'$ such that $\forall d'$ with d' label of C': (d, d') is not in the relation of $\langle C, C' \rangle$.

Alternatively, the label discarding rule can be denoted as

$$\langle C, d \rangle \leftarrow \prod_{C' \in N_0} \text{sgn} \left(\sum_{d' \in D_0} \langle C', d' \rangle \cdot \langle C, C', d, d' \rangle \right)$$

where

$$\text{sgn}(x) = \begin{cases} 1, & \text{if } x > 0 \\ 0, & \text{if } x = 0 \end{cases}$$

A shortcoming of the label discarding rule is that it computes only 2-consistency. As we have seen before, computing 2-consistency may help to find a solution of the network by restricting the search space, but one often needs additional mechanisms to actually compute a solution. We will show in the next section how to design a connectionist network for this purpose. The approach described in that section may be compared with the one in [Lange and Dyer, 1989], where signatures are used to maintain variable bindings.

7.3.2 Towards Computing Solutions

The idea is to apply the same scheme of connection as in [Cooper and Swain, 1988] but to use the potential of a 0-node to encode information about how the 0-node contributes to a solution (and not only whether it does so or not). The information is composed from the codings that are associated with the 2-nodes. In particular, we encode each 2-node by a prime number and denote this encoding by a function e from the set of 2-nodes to the set of prime numbers P:

$$e : N_0 \times N_0 \times D_0 \times D_0 \to P$$

For example, let $N_0 = \{C_1, C_2\}$ and $D_0 = \{d_1, d_2\}$, then e may be defined as follows:

$$e\langle C_1, C_1, d_1, d_1 \rangle = 2 \qquad e\langle C_1, C_2, d_1, d_1 \rangle = e\langle C_2, C_1, d_1, d_1 \rangle = 11$$
$$e\langle C_1, C_1, d_2, d_2 \rangle = 3 \qquad e\langle C_1, C_2, d_1, d_2 \rangle = e\langle C_2, C_1, d_2, d_1 \rangle = 13$$
$$e\langle C_2, C_2, d_1, d_1 \rangle = 5 \qquad e\langle C_1, C_2, d_2, d_1 \rangle = e\langle C_2, C_1, d_1, d_2 \rangle = 17$$
$$e\langle C_2, C_2, d_2, d_2 \rangle = 7 \qquad e\langle C_1, C_2, d_2, d_2 \rangle = e\langle C_2, C_1, d_2, d_2 \rangle = 19$$

Nodes such as $\langle C_1, C_1, d_1, d_2 \rangle$ with $d_1 \neq d_2$ do not make sense and therefore are omitted in the coding.

We will again use the same notation for a node and its potential, i.e., the term $\langle C_1, C_2, d_1, d_2 \rangle$, for example, may denote the connectionist node representing the relation element (d_1, d_2) of the binary constraint between C_1 and C_2, or may denote the potential of that node. The intended meaning is determined by the context.

The initial potentials of 2-nodes are identical with the ones used in [Cooper, 1989]. A 2-node $\langle C_1, C_2, d_1, d_2 \rangle$ is assigned the potential 1, if there is a pair (d_1, d_2) in the relation of the constraint between C_1 and C_2; else it is 0.

The initial potential of a 0-node $\langle C, d \rangle$ is equal to 1, if d is *not* an element of the relation of C. Otherwise, the initial potential of $\langle C, d \rangle$ is determined by the product of the codes of all 2-nodes except those that refer to the same 0-ary constraint as the given

0-node but to a different value for that constraint (i.e., a factor $e\langle C, .., d', ..\rangle$ with $d' \neq d$ does not occur in the product):

$$\langle C, d \rangle \leftarrow \prod_{\substack{C' \in N_0 \\ d' \in D_0}} e\langle C, C', d, d' \rangle \prod_{\substack{C', C'' \in N_0 \setminus \{C\} \\ d', d'' \in D_0}} \sqrt{e\langle C', C'', d', d'' \rangle}$$

The square root is due to the fact that $\langle C', C'', d', d'' \rangle$ and $\langle C'', C', d'', d' \rangle$ are identical nodes.

Instead of computing arc consistency (in which a 0-node's potential is reset to 0 if it is inconsistent), we will perform here what is called degradation:

1. A 2-node receives the potentials of its 0-nodes and computes their greatest common divisor (gcd).

2. The gcd is returned to the 0-nodes if the 2-node has potential 1; else 1 is returned.

3. A 0-node computes the least common multiples (lcm) of data coming in from 2-nodes that refer to the same 0-ary constraint, and combines these by computing their gdc.

The idea is that the potentials of 0-nodes shall reflect paths in the network that correspond to solutions of the constraint satisfaction problem. A 0-node may be on the same path as another 0-node if the 2-node between them has potential 1. We start with allowing all paths among the 0-nodes. Whenever a part of path is determined that is not admissible, i.e., the corresponding 2-node has potential 0, the path is deleted.

This means that global information about solution paths is held locally in the 0-nodes of the network. To keep this information consistent, the 2-nodes compute the gcd of the potentials of neighboring 0-nodes. The gcd reflects that piece of information neighboring 0-nodes can agree on. In order to consider alternatives, the 0-nodes compute the lcm of data that come in from 2-nodes connecting to the same 0-ary constraint, and combine the results by applying the gcd operator. The alternation between the application of gcd and lcm directly corresponds to the semantics of constraints and their constituting tuples: a constraint network may be viewed as a conjunction of constraints (therefore gcd) wheras a constraint may be viewed as disjunction of tuples (therefore lcm).

More formally, the degradation rule can be denoted as follows:

$$\langle C, d \rangle \leftarrow \gcd{}_{C' \in N_0} \text{lcm}_{d' \in D_0} (\text{out}(\langle C, C', d, d' \rangle))$$

with

$$\text{out}(\langle C, C', d, d' \rangle) = \begin{cases} \gcd(\langle C, d \rangle, \langle C', d' \rangle), & \text{if } \langle C, C', d, d' \rangle = 1 \\ 1, & \text{else} \end{cases}$$

Since the degradation rule is monotonic and discrete, and since only positive potentials occur, the network finally settles down. After that, the potentials of the 0-nodes characterize the set of solutions of the given dynamic constraint network. In particular,

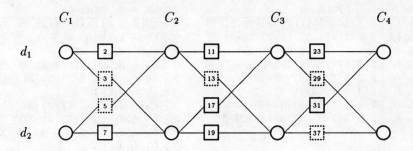

Figure 7.5: Connectionist network for a simple constraint satisfaction problem. We use circles for representing 0-nodes, boxes with solid boundary lines for 2-nodes that have potential 1, and boxes with dashed boundary lines for 2-nodes that have potential 0.

a solution is given by a subset of nodes, Z, for which the following holds:

$$\forall C \in N_0 \; \exists d \in D_0 : \langle C, d \rangle \in Z \tag{7.1}$$

(Every 0-ary constraint occurs in Z.)

$$\forall C \in N_0 \; \forall d_1, d_2 \in D_0 : \langle C, d_1 \rangle \in Z \Rightarrow \langle C, d_2 \rangle \notin Z \tag{7.2}$$

(Only one element of each 0-ary constraint is in Z.)

$$\forall C_1, C_2 \in N_0 \; \forall d_1, d_2 \in D_0 : \tag{7.3}$$
$$\langle C_1, d_1 \rangle \in Z \land \langle C_2, d_2 \rangle \in Z \Leftrightarrow \langle C_1, C_2, d_1, d_2 \rangle \in Z$$

(A 2-node is in Z if and only if the corresponding 0-nodes are in Z.)

$$\forall \langle C, d \rangle \in Z : \langle C, d \rangle \text{ is divisible by} \tag{7.4}$$
$$p = \prod_{\langle C_1, C_2, d_1, d_2 \rangle \in Z} \sqrt{e \langle C_1, C_2, d_1, d_2 \rangle}$$

(The potentials of the 0-nodes in Z are divisible by p.)

We will show in the next section that the approach is sound and complete. We will also provide some upper bound for its space complexity. Before that, however, we will illustrate our approach by a small example. Figure 7.5 shows a part of a connectionist network for a constraint problem with 0-ary constraints C_1, C_2, C_3, C_4 and binary constraints $\langle C_1, C_2 \rangle, \langle C_1, C_3 \rangle, \langle C_1, C_4 \rangle, \langle C_2, C_3 \rangle, \langle C_2, C_4 \rangle, \langle C_4, C_5 \rangle$. The following table lists the relations of the constraints:

Constraint	Relation
$\langle C_1, C_2 \rangle$	$\{(d_1, d_1), (d_2, d_2)\}$
$\langle C_2, C_3 \rangle$	$\{(d_1, d_1), (d_2, d_2), (d_2, d_1)\}$
$\langle C_3, C_4 \rangle$	$\{(d_1, d_1), (d_2, d_1)\}$

For all constraints not listed in the table, the constraint relation is equal to the domain of the constraint. For the sake of simplicity, 2-nodes that correspond to universal constraints, i.e., constraints with the domain as relation, are omitted in the example. This

0-Node	Initial Potential
$\langle C_1, d_1 \rangle$	$2 \cdot 3 \cdot 11 \cdot 13 \cdot 17 \cdot 19 \cdot 23 \cdot 29 \cdot 31 \cdot 37$
$\langle C_1, d_2 \rangle$	$5 \cdot 7 \cdot 11 \cdot 13 \cdot 17 \cdot 19 \cdot 23 \cdot 29 \cdot 31 \cdot 37$
$\langle C_2, d_1 \rangle$	$2 \cdot 5 \cdot 11 \cdot 13 \cdot 23 \cdot 29 \cdot 31 \cdot 37$
$\langle C_2, d_2 \rangle$	$3 \cdot 7 \cdot 17 \cdot 19 \cdot 23 \cdot 29 \cdot 31 \cdot 37$
$\langle C_3, d_1 \rangle$	$2 \cdot 3 \cdot 5 \cdot 7 \cdot 11 \cdot 17 \cdot 23 \cdot 29$
$\langle C_3, d_2 \rangle$	$2 \cdot 3 \cdot 5 \cdot 7 \cdot 13 \cdot 19 \cdot 31 \cdot 37$
$\langle C_4, d_1 \rangle$	$2 \cdot 3 \cdot 5 \cdot 7 \cdot 11 \cdot 13 \cdot 17 \cdot 19 \cdot 23 \cdot 31$
$\langle C_4, d_2 \rangle$	$2 \cdot 3 \cdot 5 \cdot 7 \cdot 11 \cdot 13 \cdot 17 \cdot 19 \cdot 29 \cdot 37$

2-Node	Output
$\langle C_1, C_2, d_1, d_1 \rangle$	$2 \cdot 11 \cdot 13 \cdot 23 \cdot 29 \cdot 31 \cdot 37$
$\langle C_1, C_2, d_1, d_2 \rangle$	1
$\langle C_1, C_2, d_2, d_1 \rangle$	1
$\langle C_1, C_2, d_2, d_2 \rangle$	$7 \cdot 17 \cdot 19 \cdot 23 \cdot 29 \cdot 31 \cdot 37$
$\langle C_2, C_3, d_1, d_1 \rangle$	$2 \cdot 5 \cdot 11 \cdot 23 \cdot 29$
$\langle C_2, C_3, d_1, d_2 \rangle$	1
$\langle C_2, C_3, d_2, d_1 \rangle$	$3 \cdot 7 \cdot 17 \cdot 23 \cdot 29$
$\langle C_2, C_3, d_2, d_2 \rangle$	$3 \cdot 7 \cdot 19 \cdot 31 \cdot 37$
$\langle C_3, C_4, d_1, d_1 \rangle$	$2 \cdot 3 \cdot 5 \cdot 7 \cdot 11 \cdot 17 \cdot 23$
$\langle C_3, C_4, d_1, d_2 \rangle$	1
$\langle C_3, C_4, d_2, d_1 \rangle$	$2 \cdot 3 \cdot 5 \cdot 7 \cdot 13 \cdot 19 \cdot 31$
$\langle C_3, C_4, d_2, d_2 \rangle$	1

0-Node	Potential
$\langle C_1, d_1 \rangle$	$2 \cdot 11 \cdot 13 \cdot 23 \cdot 29 \cdot 31 \cdot 37$
$\langle C_1, d_2 \rangle$	$7 \cdot 17 \cdot 19 \cdot 23 \cdot 29 \cdot 31 \cdot 37$
$\langle C_2, d_1 \rangle$	$2 \cdot 11 \cdot 23 \cdot 29$
$\langle C_2, d_2 \rangle$	$7 \cdot 17 \cdot 19 \cdot 23 \cdot 29 \cdot 31 \cdot 37$
$\langle C_3, d_1 \rangle$	$2 \cdot 3 \cdot 5 \cdot 7 \cdot 11 \cdot 17 \cdot 23$
$\langle C_3, d_2 \rangle$	$3 \cdot 7 \cdot 19 \cdot 31$
$\langle C_4, d_1 \rangle$	$2 \cdot 3 \cdot 5 \cdot 7 \cdot 11 \cdot 13 \cdot 17 \cdot 19 \cdot 23 \cdot 31$
$\langle C_4, d_2 \rangle$	1

2-Node	Output
$\langle C_1, C_2, d_1, d_1 \rangle$	$2 \cdot 11 \cdot 23 \cdot 29$
$\langle C_1, C_2, d_1, d_2 \rangle$	1
$\langle C_1, C_2, d_2, d_1 \rangle$	1
$\langle C_1, C_2, d_2, d_2 \rangle$	$7 \cdot 17 \cdot 19 \cdot 23 \cdot 29 \cdot 31 \cdot 37$
$\langle C_2, C_3, d_1, d_1 \rangle$	$2 \cdot 11 \cdot 23$
$\langle C_2, C_3, d_1, d_2 \rangle$	1
$\langle C_2, C_3, d_2, d_1 \rangle$	$7 \cdot 17 \cdot 23$
$\langle C_2, C_3, d_2, d_2 \rangle$	$7 \cdot 19 \cdot 31$
$\langle C_3, C_4, d_1, d_1 \rangle$	$2 \cdot 3 \cdot 5 \cdot 7 \cdot 11 \cdot 17 \cdot 23$
$\langle C_3, C_4, d_1, d_2 \rangle$	1
$\langle C_3, C_4, d_2, d_1 \rangle$	$3 \cdot 7 \cdot 19 \cdot 31$
$\langle C_3, C_4, d_2, d_2 \rangle$	1

Figure 7.6: Sequence of 0-node potentials and 2-node outputs (part 1).

simplification is admissible since all 0-nodes have already been connected by nonuniversal constraints, guaranteeing that inconsistent codes are removed from the potentials of the 0-nodes.

Figures 7.6 and 7.7 show a sequence of tables in which listings of 0-node potentials and 2-node outputs alternate. The sequence illustrates how the network is initialized and how it settles down. The example suggests that nodes in the center of the network ($\langle C_2, d_1 \rangle$, $\langle C_2, d_2 \rangle$, $\langle C_3, d_1 \rangle$, and $\langle C_3, d_2 \rangle$) settle down faster than nodes at the periphery ($\langle C_1, d_1 \rangle$, $\langle C_1, d_2 \rangle$, $\langle C_4, d_1 \rangle$, and $\langle C_4, d_2 \rangle$). This, however, is only because we have simplified the example and left out some connections. In a network with full connectivity, there is no distinction between center nodes and peripheral nodes; therefore, these networks settle down in a more uniform way.

0-Node	Potential		2-Node	Output
$\langle C_1, d_1 \rangle$	$2 \cdot 11 \cdot 23 \cdot 29$		$\langle C_1, C_2, d_1, d_1 \rangle$	$2 \cdot 11 \cdot 23$
$\langle C_1, d_2 \rangle$	$7 \cdot 17 \cdot 19 \cdot 23 \cdot 29 \cdot 31 \cdot 37$		$\langle C_1, C_2, d_1, d_2 \rangle$	1
$\langle C_2, d_1 \rangle$	$2 \cdot 11 \cdot 23$		$\langle C_1, C_2, d_2, d_1 \rangle$	1
$\langle C_2, d_2 \rangle$	$7 \cdot 17 \cdot 19 \cdot 23 \cdot 31$		$\langle C_1, C_2, d_2, d_2 \rangle$	$7 \cdot 17 \cdot 19 \cdot 23 \cdot 31$
$\langle C_3, d_1 \rangle$	$2 \cdot 7 \cdot 11 \cdot 17 \cdot 23$		$\langle C_2, C_3, d_1, d_1 \rangle$	$2 \cdot 11 \cdot 23$
$\langle C_3, d_2 \rangle$	$7 \cdot 19 \cdot 31$		$\langle C_2, C_3, d_1, d_2 \rangle$	1
$\langle C_4, d_1 \rangle$	$2 \cdot 3 \cdot 5 \cdot 7 \cdot 11 \cdot 17 \cdot 19 \cdot 23 \cdot 31$		$\langle C_2, C_3, d_2, d_1 \rangle$	$7 \cdot 17 \cdot 23$
$\langle C_4, d_2 \rangle$	1		$\langle C_2, C_3, d_2, d_2 \rangle$	$7 \cdot 19 \cdot 31$
			$\langle C_3, C_4, d_1, d_1 \rangle$	$2 \cdot 7 \cdot 11 \cdot 17 \cdot 23$
			$\langle C_3, C_4, d_1, d_2 \rangle$	1
			$\langle C_3, C_4, d_2, d_1 \rangle$	$7 \cdot 19 \cdot 31$
			$\langle C_3, C_4, d_2, d_2 \rangle$	1

0-Node	Final Potential
$\langle C_1, d_1 \rangle$	$2 \cdot 11 \cdot 23$
$\langle C_1, d_2 \rangle$	$7 \cdot 17 \cdot 19 \cdot 23 \cdot 31$
$\langle C_2, d_1 \rangle$	$2 \cdot 11 \cdot 23$
$\langle C_2, d_2 \rangle$	$7 \cdot 17 \cdot 19 \cdot 23 \cdot 31$
$\langle C_3, d_1 \rangle$	$2 \cdot 7 \cdot 11 \cdot 17 \cdot 23$
$\langle C_3, d_2 \rangle$	$7 \cdot 19 \cdot 31$
$\langle C_4, d_1 \rangle$	$2 \cdot 7 \cdot 11 \cdot 17 \cdot 19 \cdot 23 \cdot 31$
$\langle C_4, d_2 \rangle$	1

Figure 7.7: Sequence of 0-node potentials and 2-node outputs (part 2).

7.3.3   Termination, Soundness, and Completeness

The kernel of our approach is the degradation rule as introduced in the previous section, which, on a more abstract level, may be denoted as follows:

$$\langle C, d \rangle \leftarrow \text{degrade}(\ldots, \langle C, d \rangle, \ldots)$$

In this context, two observations are important: first, degrade is composed of gcd's and lcm's in such a way that factors are deleted from $\langle C, d \rangle$ rather than added, and second, the number of factors with which $\langle C, d \rangle$ is initialized is finite. This implies that degradation terminates, independently of the given constraint satisfaction problem:

Prop. 13 (Termination of Degradation)
Given a connectionist network as defined above. Then, the application of the degradation rule terminates.

We will call the result of applying degradation iteratively until no further changes occur the degraded network. The potentials of the 0-nodes of the degraded network specify the solutions of the corresponding dynamic constraint network. This is captured in the following propositions:

Prop. 14 (Soundness of Degradation)
Given a dynamic constraint network and its corresponding degraded connectionist network as defined above. Let Z be a subset of nodes with properties 7.1–7.4. Then, Z represents a solution of the dynamic constraint network.

Proof: Let us assume that there is a subset of nodes, Z, for which the above conditions hold but which does not represent a solution of the constraint satisfaction problem. This means that the tuple suggested by Z violates at least one constraint of the dynamic network.

Case 1: Suppose the arity of the violated constraint, C, is equal to 0. Then, let $\langle C, d \rangle$ be the 0-node in Z corresponding to C. Since C is violated, the potential of $\langle C, d \rangle$ is 1. This contradicts the requirement of each 0-node potential being divisible by p (cf. property 7.4).

Case 2: Suppose the arity of the violated constraint, $\langle C_1, C_2 \rangle$, is equal to 2. Then, let $\langle C_1, C_2, d_1, d_2 \rangle$ be the 2-node in Z corresponding to C. Since C is violated, the potential of $\langle C_1, C_2, d_1, d_2 \rangle$ is 0. Due to the initialization scheme, the potential of a node $\langle C_1, d_1' \rangle$ with $d_1' \neq d_1$ does not contain the factor $e\langle C_1, C_2, d_1, d_2 \rangle$; the same holds for $\langle C_2, d_2' \rangle$ with $d_2' \neq d_2$. Since the potential of $\langle C_1, C_2, d_1, d_2 \rangle$ is 0 and since no other node can provide the factor $e\langle C_1, C_2, d_1, d_2 \rangle$, this factor is neither in the potential of $\langle C_1, d_1 \rangle$ nor in the potential of $\langle C_2, d_2 \rangle$, i.e., these potentials are not divisible by $e\langle C_1, C_2, d_1, d_2 \rangle$. Therefore, they are also not divisible by p (p defined as above), which contradicts property 7.4.
□

Prop. 15 (Completeness of Degradation)
Given a dynamic constraint network and its corresponding degraded connectionist network as defined above. Let S be a solution of the dynamic constraint network. Then, there is a subset Z of nodes with properties 7.1–7.4 that represents S.

Proof: Each solution of a given dynamic constraint network defines a subset of nodes, Z, for which properties 7.1, 7.2, and 7.3 hold trivally. Thus, it remains to be shown:

$$\forall \langle C, d \rangle \in Z : \langle C, d \rangle \text{ is divisible by } p = \prod_{\langle C_1, C_2, d_1, d_2 \rangle \in Z} \sqrt{e \langle C_1, C_2, d_1, d_2 \rangle}$$

Since Z represents a solution of the dynamic constraint network, the potentials of all 2-nodes in Z are equal to 1. This means that the potential of each 0-node in Z is divisible by the code of any 2-node in Z, i.e., the potential of each 0-node in Z is divisible by p. $\square$

With that, we have shown the soundness and completeness of our approach, i.e., the one-to-one relationship between solutions of a given constraint satisfaction problem and special subsets of 0-nodes in the corresponding connectionist network. We will now discuss the complexity of our approach.

7.3.4 Space Complexity

Let n be the number of 0-ary constraints of the given constraint satisfaction problem ($n = |N_0|$), and let m be the number of values in their domain ($m = |D_0|$). Since $N_2 = \{\langle C_1, C_2 \rangle \mid C_1, C_2 \in N_0, C_1 \neq C_2\}$ and $D_2 = D_0 \times D_0$, we have:

$$|N_2| = \sum_{i=1}^{n-1} i = \frac{n(n-1)}{2} \qquad\qquad |D_2| = m^2$$

Hence, the number of nodes can be estimated as follows:

Number of 0-nodes:	$O(mn)$
Number of 2-nodes:	$O(m^2n^2)$
Total number of nodes:	$O(m^2n^2)$

In addition, we have to consider the local space that is required for storing the Gödel numbers. Each 0-node potential is the product of at most $O(m^2n^2)$ factors, corresponding to the 2-nodes of the network. These factors could be represented by bit vectors, which facilitates the gcd and lcm operations, reducing them to intersection und union operations. This means that we need additional space of magnitude $O(m^2n^2)$ for each 0-node, i.e., $O(m^3n^3)$ additional space in total.

7.4 Summarizing

We have shown in this chapter how filtering can be performed in parallel. We started with a simple scheme for implementing filtering and filtering with tagging on multiprocessors. Then, we introduced how an arbitrary binary constraint satisfaction problem, i.e., a set of 0-ary and binary dynamic constraints, can be transformed into a connectionist network consisting of 0-nodes and 2-nodes. 2-nodes are initialized with either 1 or 0, depending on whether they correspond to an admissible value combination or an inconsistent one; 0-nodes are initialized with a Gödel number, representing the possible paths of solutions.

Chapter 8

Optimization Approaches

The approaches described in the preceding chapters 5–7 do the job of finding *some* solution to a given dynCSP. However, this is not always what we want; there are cases where there is a whole lot of solutions to a dynamic network, and you are in search for a "good" or even an optimal one, regarding some quality measure. So if there are a great many solutions to a dynCSP (and only then in our context) optimizing the generated solution is a natural question. We have already seen a class of examples for this case: constraint relaxation as described in chapter 4; associating qualities with solutions, however, is not restricted to relaxation but can be used more generally.

Given a metric on solutions to a dynCSP, finding an optimal or sufficiently good solution can obviously be seen as a problem of combinatorial optimization. There is a wealth of literature about that field, and there are a lot of intensively studied algorithms and approaches, nearly all of which we will omit here, except for two: simulated annealing and Boltzmann machines. There are four reasons why we have chosen them for being presented here:

- There are nice applications of approaching practical constraint problems with simulated annealing, e.g., [Bolz and Wittur, 1990] and Boltzmann machines, e.g., [Adorf and Johnston, 1990] (well, something very similar to Boltzmann machines: Hopfield networks).

- There is theoretical work [Pinkas, 1991] on the relationship between symmetric neural networks (to which Boltzmann machines belong) and propositional nonmonotonic reasoning (which, as we have shown in section 4.4, is closely related to constraint relaxation).

- Simulated annealing and Boltzmann machines are two different but closely related approaches.

- They can be implemented on the whole spectrum from serial to massively parallel machines.

In this chapter, we can only give a sketch of simulated annealing and Boltzmann machines themselves; for an overview of the many theoretical and practical results about them see, e.g., [Aarts and Korst, 1989], from which the material presented here is abstracted as far as it is not specific for dynamic constraint issues. We will see that simulated annealing is a bit questionable as an approach for solving dynCSPs: It essentially assumes that for finding good solutions, finding *some* solution is a cheap operation. This is a very strong assumption in general. However, if you are in doubt as to whether the general practical relevance of the simulated annealing approach as presented, just see it as a didactic preparation for the Boltzmann machine approach presented in section 8.2.

8.1   Simulated Annealing

To start with, the funny name of simulated annealing stems from an analogy to heating up and cooling down solids to have them crystallize in perfect lattices; this is unimportant here. The idea behind simulated annealing is as follows. There are a couple of approaches to combinatorial optimization that involve randomly generating an arbitrary solution and improving it by somewhat local changes within that solution, yielding a "neighboring" solution. Take as an example a dynCSP:

- Assume that the dynamic network N involved has a generating set M.

- Find an arbitrary solution $(d_1, \ldots, d_n)$ of N as the currently best solution S^*.

- Then a local change to this solution could be achieved by arbitrarily selecting, say, three dynamic constraints from M, assigning to them, their dependent constraints, and the respective components of constraints they depend on, respectively, their original domains, and solving the resulting dynCSP. If the new solution S is not worse than the currently best one, it becomes the new S^*.

- Continue the previous step until some stop criterion is fulfilled.

Note that the concept of a neighboring solution is quite far-fetched for dynCSPs in general; it should prove workable, however, if there are many solutions for a dynCSP given, as we assumed for this section. The very procedure to generate neighboring solutions proposed here is a bit dubious and might be replaced by any other one for practical purposes. The point is: there must be *some* procedure of this kind.

All hill-climbing-like approaches as the one described here suffer from a serious theoretical problem: depending on the choice of the initial solution and the local changes made to it, they may end up in only *locally* optimal solutions S^*—it may be impossible to improve the currently best solution by local changes, even though there are better solutions to the original problem.

Simulated annealing is one of the approaches involving local improvements, but it circumvents this problem in the following way. Avoiding to get stuck in a non-global maximum is assured by accepting a deterioration in what is taken to be the currently best solution S^* from time to time, that may (but need not) lead us to a better solution on the long run. However, accepting worse solutions as currently best must *also* be limited in order to guarantee finding a good solution in the end. The strategy here is that the probability of accepting a solution worse than S^* as the new S^* decreases with the degree of deterioration and, even more important, the run time of the algorithm. The formal criterion is as follows. Let f be the function determining a penalty to a solution, and let S be a newly generated solution worse than S^*, i.e., $f(S) > f(S^*)$. Then S is accepted as the new S^* if

$$\exp(\frac{f(S^*) - f(S)}{c_k}) > \text{random}[0, 1) \tag{8.1}$$

where random generates a random number with a uniform distribution over its argument interval. Practically, the factor c_0 to be started with is a positive real number close to 1, and each c_{k+1} is less than c_k, asymptotically approximating 0. A typical recipe for calculating c_{k+1} is

$$c_{k+1} = \alpha c_k$$

where a typical α is between 0.8 and 0.99. As a result, the acceptance of a deterioration gets less and less probable over time. You just have to define after how many runs of the algorithm you take a new c_k; this is done by using an array l_k. The simulated annealing algorithm, then, reads as shown in Figure 8.1.[1]

Now what about the result of the algorithm? Exactly, how good is the S^* returned? It can be proven that the algorithm asymptotically returns a globally optimal solution for the right choice of the parameters. There is just one problem: it may have to generate a neighboring solution infinitely often within that process, even for finite sets of solutions. That is clearly intolerable: even enumerating *all* solutions and picking a globally best one would be more efficient (if it is allowed to use this term here). However, it can be proven (and actually has been proven in [Aarts and Korst, 1989, section 4.2]) that the simulated annealing algorithm will find a close to optimal solution in $O(\ln |\mathcal{S}|)$ time, where $\mathcal{S}$ is the set of all solutions to the given problem, presumed that c_0 and the parameters l_k are set correctly, the calculation of c_{k+1} in step 2 is done correctly, and the stop criterion is right.

The O-notation hides the cost of generating neighboring solutions, which is assumed to take constant time. It is reasonable to assume that this cost will be high for arbitrary dynCSPs such that the time consumption of finding a near to optimal solution will be considerable in practice, which is confirmed by the findings of Bolz and Wittur [1990] for solving an ordinary CSP with simulated annealing. But what else can we expect? We know that solving CSPs and hence dynCSPs is NP-hard, and so we should not be surprised if searching for an *optimal*—or close to optimal—solution is not easy.

Moreover, *every* approach involving the generation and comparison of many solutions would cause the cost of generating them—not only simulated annealing. If this proves to be too expensive for a given dynCSP, but the goal of optimizing is retained, then there is only one alternative: optimizing during the generation of *one* solution. This could be done in a best-first variant of the algorithm for chronological backtracking: the selection of constraints and values in steps 4a and 4b could take the current penalty into account, instead of the heuristics we talked about in section 5.2, potentially sacrificing speed for quality of the solution. There is no way around the tradeoff between these two features and hence around the decision which feature you want to stress.

---

[1]Note that the if–then–else construct in step 1b of algorithm 8.1 is unnecessarily complex; in our case, the else-if line corresponding to unequation 8.1 would have been sufficient as the exp function returns a value ≥ 1 for positive c_k if $f(S) \leq f(S^*)$. For clarity, we stick to this form of the algorithm adopted from [Aarts and Korst, 1989].

Algorithm 5 (Simulated Annealing)
Given

- *a dynCSP N,*

- *a procedure to generate a neighboring solution to a given solution of N,*

- *an arbitrary solution S^* of N,*

- *a measure function f for determining a penalty for a solution of N (the smaller $f(S)$, the better S),*

- *initial values for c_0 and l_0 as described above.*

loop for *k* **from** 0

　　1. **loop repeat** l_k

　　　　(a) generate a neighboring solution S of S^*;

　　　　(b) **if** $f(S) \leq f(S^*)$
　　　　　　　then $S^* \leftarrow S$
　　　　　　　else if $\exp(\frac{f(S^*)-f(S)}{c_k}) > random[0,1)$
　　　　　　　then $S^* \leftarrow S$

　　2. calculate c_{k+1} and l_{k+1}

until *stop criterion;*

return S^*

Figure 8.1: A simulated annealing algorithm for finding a good solution of a dynCSP.

8.2 Connectionist Optimization: Boltzmann Machines

We now come to discussing the realization of dynamic constraint networks with Boltzmann machines, which are in principle a connectionist approach. From our pragmatical point of view, however, Boltzmann machines are just an approach to optimization, and therefore they bear a strong connection to simulated annealing as described in the previous section 8.1. There are, however, deeper theoretical and practical similarities between these two approaches; the reader is referred to the introduction by Aarts and Korst [1989] to explore them in more detail. Like our description of simulated annealing, the one of Boltzmann machines which follows is abstracted (and simplified) from theirs. Note that we will use some basic Boltzmann machine concepts only; for example, we will not talk about the learning capabilities of them nor use them. Our translation of dynamic constraint networks into Boltzmann machines is similar to the one of constraint networks into Hopfield networks proposed by [Johnston and Adorf, 1989; Adorf and Johnston, 1990], their work, however, not dealing with relaxation issues.

A Boltzmann machine is a graph $B = (U, K)$, where U is the finite set of *units* and K is is a set of unordered pairs of elements of U, the *connections*, each connection written as $\{u, v\}$, for $u, v \in U$. K includes all *bias connections*, i.e., connections connecting a unit with itself. In short: $\{\{u, u\} \mid u \in U\} \subset K$. The units are binary valued, i.e., they are either *on* or *off*, which is represented as 1 and 0, respectively. A *configuration* of a Boltzmann machine is a 0-1-vector of length $|U|$ describing the state of each unit. If k is a configuration, $k(u)$ denotes the state of u in k.

Connections are either active or passive, which is important as configurations will be measured by the sum of weights associated with active connections. A connection between u und v is *active* in a configuration k if both connected units are on, i.e., if $k(u) \cdot k(v) = 1$; else it is *passive*. Every connection $\{u, v\}$ has an associated *connection strength* $s_{\{u,v\}} \in I\!\!R$, to be interpreted as the desirability that $\{u, v\}$ is active. The strength of a bias connection $\{u, u\}$ is called the *bias* of u.

The desirability of a whole configuration k, expressed in terms of a *consensus function* is the sum of the strengths of all active connections; hence the consensus function $\kappa(k)$ looks as follows:

$$\kappa(k) = \sum_{\{u,v\} \in K} s_{\{u,v\}} \cdot k(u) \cdot k(v).$$

The objective of a Boltzmann machine is to find a configuration with a globally maximal consensus function.

It is time now for an example, and as the objective of this section is to show how solving dynamic constraint networks can be formulated in terms of Boltzmann machines, we use the transformation of a dynamic constraint network, namely the one shown in figure 8.2. We will generalize this transformation later.

The idea of the transformation is to have one unit per every relation element of every dynamic constraint (often called the unit/value principle [Feldman and Ballard, 1982]). So to transform the network in figure 8.2, we get, for instance, two units $y = c, y = d$ as a transformation of the 0-ary constraint y and also two units, respectively, as transformations of all the other constraints. Concerning the connections, there are, firstly, the bias

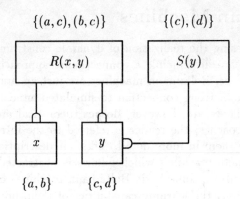

Figure 8.2: The abstract example for this section: a simple network consisting of four dynamic constraints.

connections connecting each unit with itself. Secondly, there must be a link between two units u, v if u, v represent relation elements of constraints C_1, C_2, respectively, and C_1 is a dependent of C_2; there are only connections corresponding to fitting pairs of relation and one argument (like the connection between the units corresponding to $S = (c)$ and $y = c$), called *positive* connections. And thirdly, there is a connection between every pair of units representing different elements of the same relation—like $S = (c)$ and $S = (d)$; these are called *intra-relation* connections. The Boltzmann machine contains only the positive, intra-relation, and bias connections. The machine corresponding to the example then looks like that shown in figure 8.3.

The connections are associated with the following strengths: positive connections have strength 1, intra-relation connections -3, and bias connections 0. Let k_0 be the following configuration

$$k_0(u) = \begin{cases} 1 & \text{if } u \in \{R = (a, c), S = (c), S = (d), x = a, y = c\} \\ 0 & \text{else} \end{cases}$$

then the consensus function $\kappa(k_0) = 0$.

The objective of a Boltzmann machine is to find a global maximum of the consensus function. In general, a Boltzmann machine can be understood as working sequentially, where units are allowed to change their states only one unit at a time, and in parallel. We will only consider the sequential mode of operation here. As before, we refer to [Aarts and Korst, 1989] for further information.

The idea how to arrive at a global maximum is essentially the same as in simulated annealing: take an arbitrary configuration as the recent one; generate a neighboring one (by changing the state of one unit); accept it as the recent configuration with some probability depending on the difference of consensus compared to the recent configuration and on run time of the procedure; continue.

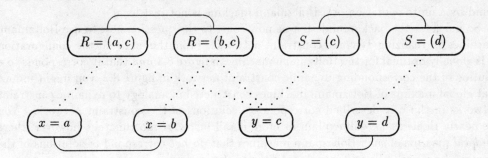

Figure 8.3: The Boltzmann machine corresponding to the constraint network in figure 8.2. Positive connections are depicted as dotted lines, intra-relation connections as open ovals, and bias connections are omitted for clearness.

To sketch this briefly, given a configuration k, we define a *neighboring configuration* k_u as the one obtained from k by changing the state of the unit u. Noticing that $k_u(u) = 1 - k(u)$ and $k_u(v) = k(v)$ for $v \neq u$, it is easy to verify that the *difference in consensus* between k and k_u, which is denoted by $\Delta\kappa_k(u)$ and equals $\kappa(k_u) - \kappa(k)$, is obtained by

$$\Delta\kappa_k(u) = (1 - 2k(u)) \cdot \left(s_{\{u,u\}} + \sum_{\{u,v\} \in K_u} s_{\{u,v\}} \cdot k(v) \right)$$

where K_u denotes the set of connections incident with u, excluding $\{u,u\}$. A configuration k is locally maximal if $\Delta\kappa_k(u) \leq 0$ for all units u, i.e., if its consensus cannot be increased by a *single* state change.

For example, the configuration k_0 we have been talking about earlier has no maximal consensus value: switching off the unit $S = (d)$ leads to the following configuration

$$k_1(u) = \begin{cases} 1 & \text{if } u \in \{R = (a,c), S = (c), x = a, y = c\} \\ 0 & \text{else} \end{cases}$$

which has a consensus value of 3; it obviously is locally maximal, and it is even globally maximal.

Given a configuration k, assume that neighboring configurations k_u are generated with equal probabilities for all u. The *acceptance criterion* to accept k_u as the recent configuration is

$$\frac{1}{1 + \exp \frac{-\Delta\kappa_k(u)}{c_t}} > random[0,1),$$

where $c_t > 0$ and converges to 0 for increasing t. Note the similarity to the acceptance criterion for simulated annealing in equation 8.1.

Like for simulated annealing, it can be proven (and *is* proven in [Aarts and Korst, 1989, Theorem 8.1]) that the configuration chosen asymptotically converges to a globally optimal one as c_t converges to 0. On the other hand, there is no guarantee that a maximum found by a finite operation of a Boltzmann machine is not just local.

So much for the background. Let us now come to the question how to use Boltzmann machines for realizing dynamic constraint networks. From the fact that the configuration k_1 is globally optimal for the Boltzmann machine in figure 8.3 *and* that it corresponds to a solution of the corresponding dynamic constraint network in figure 8.2, you might induce that global maxima of Boltzmann machines constructed in analogy to dynamic constraint networks in the way described correspond to solutions of the constraint networks. You are nearly right, as we will explain in more detail below. Unfortunately, however, there are *local* maxima of such Boltzmann machines that do *not* correspond to solutions of the constraint network. As an example take the configuration

$$k_2(u) = \begin{cases} 1 & \text{if } u \in \{y = d, S = (d)\} \\ 0 & \text{else} \end{cases}$$

k_2 is locally maximal; there are neighboring configurations (e.g., changing the state of $x = a$ or $x = b$) with a difference in consensus of 0, but no one with a positive difference. On the other hand, k_2 does not correspond to a solution of the associated dynamic constraint network.

When using Boltzmann machines for solving combinatorial optimization problems, it is usually required that the consensus function be *feasible,* i.e., that all local maxima of the Boltzmann machine correspond to solutions of the problem. As we have seen, κ is not feasible. This might cause a problem when using a Boltzmann machine as a realization of a constraint network because one is only guaranteed to find a *locally* optimal solution in finite time, and if this does not correspond to finding a solution to the original problem, namely, the dynCSP, we might ask of what value the transformation of dynCSPs to Boltzmann machines actually is.

How to get out of that? Either we could try to find another transformation and a feasible consensus function. Or we could look for an appropriate interpretation of local maxima of Boltzmann machines; and this is what we are going to do because we like the relatively close correspondence between dynamic constraint networks and Boltzmann machines constructed as described.

To start with, let us define a corresponding Boltzmann machine for a dynamic constraint network. The way to generate it is very similar to the procedure used to transform the network in figure 8.2 into the Boltzmann machine in figure 8.3; the difference is that we now want to be able to handle *relax* constraints in the network properly.[2] We assume that all *relax* constraints involve a finite number of *numerical* penalties. Moreover, we assume that all dependents of all dynamic constraints in the networks to follow must be pairwise disjoint, i.e., for all $\delta(C) = \{C_1, \ldots, C_k\}$, we require $C_i \neq C_j$ for $i \neq j$. This assumption is in fact not restrictive as every network violating it can be transformed into a fitting different one by copying and renaming the appropriate dynamic constraints.

Def. 18 (Corresponding Boltzmann machine)
Let N be a dynamic constraint network. If N contains relax *constraints $C_1, \ldots, C_r$ with*

---

[2]A note for those knowledgeable in the area of Boltzmann machines: we use the term relaxation in the sense of constraint relaxation as introduced in chapter 4, which is obviously different from its usual sense in the context of Boltzmann machines.

relations $R_1, \ldots, R_r$, let p_{max} be the maximum of the penalties occurring in the **relax** *constraints, let $\bar{p}$ be an upper bound to p_{max}, i.e., $p_{max} < \bar{p}$, and let s be an upper bound for the sum of all penalties of all* relax *constraints. (We will use $s = p_{max} \cdot \sum_{i=1}^{r} |R_i|$ in the following.)*

The corresponding Boltzmann machine $B_N = (U_N, K_N)$ is constructed in the following way.

1. *The set U_N of units includes one unit per element of every relation of every dynamic constraint of N, and it includes no other units.*

2. *Let C be a constraint in N, C' its ith dependent, let $(r_1, \ldots, r_m), (s_1, \ldots, s_m) \in R_C$, and $r' \in R_{C'}$. The set K_N of connections includes the following and no other connections:*

   - Bias Connections.

   - Positive Connections. *These are the connections between all pairs $\{u, v\}$ of units corresponding to fitting pairs of relation elements and arguments, i.e., for an $i \in \{1, \ldots, m\}$:*

     u corresponds to $(r_1, \ldots, r_m), v$ corresponds to r' and $r' = r_i$

   - Intra-relation Connections. *Connections between all pairs $\{u, v\}$ of units corresponding to different elements of the same relation, i.e.,*

     u corresponds to $(r_1, \ldots, r_m), v$ corresponds to $(s_1, \ldots, s_m)$, and $(r_1, \ldots, r_m) \neq (s_1, \ldots, s_m)$

3. *The connection strengths are set as follows:*

   - *The positive connections have strength $\bar{p}$.*

   - *The intra-relation connections have strength $-(c + \varepsilon) \cdot \bar{p}$, where $c \geq 1$ is the maximal number of positive connections a unit of the Boltzmann machine B_N is involved in, and $\varepsilon > 0$ is some real constant.*

   - *The bias connection of a unit corresponding to other than* relax *constraint elements has strength 0.*

   - *The bias connection of a unit corresponding to an element of a* relax *constraint with a penalty p has strength $\frac{\bar{p} - p - \varepsilon'}{s}$ for some real ε such that $\bar{p} - p_{max} > \varepsilon' > 0$.*

Let us briefly look at an example, namely, the one for placing a desk, a bookcase, and a terminal table into an office corner, which we used in section 4.2 and which is sketched in figure 4.5. We do not sketch the corresponding Boltzmann machine, and we recommend that you do not either, unless you are interested in designing new wallpaper. To deter, we recommend that you figure out how many units you need for representing a single 2D-composition-table constraint. (The way how to construct such a machine should be clear by the definitions and examples already presented, and actually doing so is the sort of work one should let computers do, not humans.)

However, let us think about the parameters. First, the maximum of positive connections a unit is involved in is 6, derived from the O_1/O_2 constraints each depending on 4 composition table constraints and having 2 dependents. The cardinality of the *relax-d/t* constraint is 2 as it allows the penalties 0 and 2; let us assume that the other five *relax* constraints have a cardinality of 6, allowing the penalties $0,\ldots,5$. We then get—or choose, respectively—the following parameter values:

$$
\begin{aligned}
c &= 6 \\
p_{max} &= 5 \\
\overline{p} &= 6 \\
s &= 160 \\
\varepsilon &= 1 \\
\varepsilon' &= \tfrac{1}{2}
\end{aligned}
$$

Given these values, the biases for the two units representing the *relax-d/t* constraint, for example, are $\frac{3.5}{160}, \frac{5.5}{160}$, respectively. The strenghts for positive and intra-relation connections are $6, -42$, respectively.

Remember that we have discussed two solutions for the dynamic constraint network in section 4.2 that were characterized by the following relation elements:

1. *desk/bookcase* : $(5, \langle \preceq, \sqsubset \rangle)$ 2.   *desk/bookcase* : $(0, \langle \sqsubset, \succ \rangle)$
    table/bookcase : $(3, \langle \sqsupset, \preceq \rangle)$ *table/bookcase* : $(0, \langle \sqsubset, \succ \rangle)$
    desk/table : $(2, \langle \Leftarrow, \succ \rangle)$ *desk/table* : $(2, \langle \preceq, \sqsupset \rangle)$

Every configuration of the corresponding Boltzmann machine that corresponds to a solution involves 36 active positive connections and no active intra-relation connection. In the first solution, the contribution of the biases of units corresponding to the *relax* constraints to the consensus function is

$$
\frac{3 \cdot 5.5 + 3.5 + 2.5 + 0.5}{160} = \frac{23}{160}
$$

and it is $\frac{31}{160}$ in the second solution. This yields consensus values of $216\frac{23}{160}$ and $216\frac{31}{160}$, respectively, of the configurations corresponding to the two solutions.

In the example, you can see that biases of the *relax* constraints contribute only very little to the overall consensus of a configuration. This can lead to problems with the convergence behavior of corresponding Boltzmann machines: If configurations corresponding to solutions of a largely different quality differ only marginally in their consensuses, then the probability that the Boltzmann machine will prefer the configuration corresponding to the very good solution is less than it would be if the configurations had much different consensuses. We will not pursue this problem further, but you should keep it in mind if you want to use Boltzmann machines as an implementation model for solving constraint relaxation problems practically.

Note that the example transformation we used to get the Boltzmann machine in figure 8.3 is a special case of the one now defined. Consequently, the consensus function is still not feasible under the transformation just described. However, by the very construction of B_N, we can tell whether a given local maximum of the Boltzmann machine corresponds to a solution of N. This is elaborated on in the following two propositions the proofs of which should clarify why the connection strengths in definition 18 are set the way they are.

Prop. 16 (Necessary condition for solution)
Let N be a dynamic constraint network, l the number of dependency links in N, B_N the corresponding Boltzmann machine, k a configuration of B_N, and $\overline{p}$ an upper bound of the penalties of all relax *constraints in N as defined in definition 18.*

If k corresponds to a solution of N, then for the value $\kappa(k)$ of the consensus function:

$$\kappa(k) \geq \overline{p} \cdot l \tag{8.2}$$

Proof: As we have assumed that all dependents of a dynamic constraint in N are different, l positive connections, each of strength $\overline{p}$, are active in k. By construction of B_N, no intra-relation connections are active in k, so that 8.2 follows.
□

The converse of proposition 16 is also true: every configuration k of B_N for which the inequality (8.2) holds, is a solution of N. And, more important, every such k is locally maximal.

Prop. 17 (Sufficient condition for solution)
Let $N, B_N, l, k, \overline{p}$ be defined as in proposition 16.

If $\kappa(k) \geq \overline{p} \cdot l$, then k corresponds to a solution of the dynamic constraint network N, and k is locally optimal in B_N

Proof: Firstly, note that the sum of all bias connection strengths in B_N is less than $\overline{p}$. So, by definition of the connection strengths, k must involve activating at least l different positive connections, where a solution of N corresponds to activating *exactly* l of these, by construction of B_N.

Assume that m, where $m > l$, positive connections are active in k. By construction of B_N, this involves activating at least $m - l$ intra-relation connections, each of weight $-(c + \varepsilon)\overline{p}$. Because the sum of biases is less than $\overline{p}$, this yields a consensus value smaller than $\overline{p} \cdot l$, contradicting the assumption in the proposition. So, k corresponds to a solution of N.

Now assume that k corresponds to a solution of N, i.e., it involves activating l positive connections, and assume further that $\kappa(k_u) > \kappa(k)$ by a state change of u, i.e., k is not locally optimal. As k corresponds to a solution of N, deactivating an active unit decreases the consensus. So u must be active in k_u. As k corresponds to a solution of N, activating u activates at least one intra-relation connection. By construction of B_N and by the fact that k corresponds to a solution of N, u cannot activate additional positive connections. As the highest possible bias is smaller that the negative strength of an intra-relation connection, the consensus decreases. Hence k is locally optimal.
□

The converse of the local optimality part of proposition 17 would imply feasibility of κ and hence cannot be true; i.e., there may be locally optimal configurations k where $\kappa(k) < l \cdot \overline{p}$. The configuration κ_2 above is an example.

There is another property which one would like a consensus function κ to have: given two solutions S, S' of N such that $m(S) < m(S')$ for a given metric m, then one would expect $\kappa(k) < \kappa(k')$ where k, k' are the configurations corresponding to S, S' in B_N. A consensus function for which this property holds is called *order preserving* [Aarts and Korst, 1989], and it holds for κ in the office corner furnishing example using the sum of all values of all *relax* constraints as the metric in the dynamic constraint network.

However, order preservingness does not only depend on the consensus function in the Boltzman machine in question but also on the metric in the problem space. In section 4.3 we have been talking of another metric resulting in that relaxing any number of constraints with penalty $p - 1$ is preferred to relaxing one constraint with penalty p. The κ from definition 18 is obviously *not* order preserving for this metric. So, if there is not *the* natural metric on the solution space of your original problem, you can hardly expect that one single consensus function mirrors any of them in the corresponding Boltzmann machine.

To end this rather lengthy section, we will come back to the problem that κ is not feasible. We have argued above that this may be impractical as we cannot guarantee a Boltzmann machine to deliver a global optimum, and if not every local optimum corresponds to a solution to the original dynCSP, we cannot be sure about what we have gained by a transformation of a dynCSP into a Boltzmann machine. However, the situation looks a bit more friendly now. The propositions 16 and 17 state a necessary and sufficient condition for a configuration to correspond to a solution of the dynCSP: it must be a local optimum satisfying the inequality (8.2).

If this should not suffice as a criterion for all practical purposes, then there is an alternative. Using the idea of constraint relaxation and some new value $?$ to be added to all domains, you could define for a given network N a "closure" dynamic constraint network N', in which every partial solution, i.e., a tuple consisting of locally compatible values where missing values are filled up with $?$s, is a solution which gets a penalty corresponding to the number of involved $?$s. It is easily verified—but we will not do so here—that every local optimum of B_N, i.e., the Boltzmann machine corresponding to the original constraint problem, corresponds to a solution of N', where missing values are filled up with $?$s. We have in fact seen an example for that: the configuration k_2 corresponds to the solution $(y = d, S = (d), x = R =?)$ in the hypothetical "closure" dynamic constraint network of the one in figure 8.2.

8.3   Conclusion: A Perspective of Optimization

In this chapter, we have viewed constraint satisfaction as an optimization process. It is obvious that this is possible for constraint relaxation where the issue is finding good or optimal solutions. However, as we have seen, optimization approaches can also be used for "usual" dynCSPs as there is in fact no distinction in principle between "usual" dynamic networks and those with relaxation. In this case, the Boltzmann machine would just serve as a means for generating one solution at random. You may be in doubt whether using a Boltzmann machine just to find a solution of a dynamic network is more efficient than using backtracking or filtering with tagging. However, even—or particularly?—in practical problems, you cannot be sure that your dynCSP has a solution anyway, and in such a case the output of the corresponding Boltzmann machine, which can after all be interpreted as a partial solution of the dynamic network, may be a little more helpful than the mere failing of a backtracking or tagging algorithm.

The point is that we feel the 0-1-behavior of "classical" constraint reasoning algorithms like backtracking or tagging which either find a solution or do nothing if there is no solution (except for consuming computation time) may be inappropriate sometimes. It should be possible to express the difference between "good" and "bad" solutions, and there should be some mechanism allowing constraint reasoning systems to gracefully degrade on inconsistent problems. The theoretical behavior of the algorithms presented in this chapter, particularly of the corresponding Boltzmann machine, might be a step in this direction. Maybe that using the Boltzmann machine implementation of dynamic constraint networks *as presented* yields, first of all, a very ungraceful degradation in computing time, it is true. However, we think that further work in this direction might provide more realistical approaches to constraint reasoning on the long run.

Chapter 9

Instead of a Conclusion

The purpose of this whole text is to introduce a variety of concepts, algorithms, and realizations around the notion of dynamic constraints. However, instead of summarizing the essentials of dynamic constraint reasoning in this final chapter, we want to present another dessert. Those readers who are on diet should skip this chapter; those who are looking for a summary should read the introduction chapter again.

The dessert consists of some additional remarks on the domain of spatial reasoning, which was just our demo domain here. Now, we want to change the perspective and briefly discuss how our form of spatial reasoning is located in the landscape of spatial reasoning, what limitations it has, and how serious one can take it. The discussion is directed by a historical point of view.

As pointed out in chapter 2, our form of spatial reasoning stems from the domain of temporal reasoning, especially Allen's relational temporal logic. In fact, spatial reasoning as performed in this text *is* reasoning à la Allen, just extended to higher dimensions which are to be interpreted as spatial. As a consequence, our formalism allows only for Allen relations between a typically finite number of individuals that are to be interpreted as names of spatial intervals. These names may be highly suggestive like [5.3, 16], but they are just names of "black boxes" and thus do not allow, for example, to reason about the extensions of spatial objects.

The absence of such a kind of reasoning, i.e., the handling of spatial objects as "black boxes", leads us to something else our approach is lacking. Considering a paper like [Shoham and McDermott, 1988], one sees that problems like the qualification problem, the (extended) prediction problem, the frame problem, or the persistence problem play an important role in the area of temporal reasoning. Especially the persistence problem has an obvious counterpart in spatial reasoning. Take as an example a coordinate in space of which you know that it has the property of being located in Germany. It makes perfect sense to deduce from that, that neighboring points share this property, i.e., to assume spatial persistence.

In parenthesis, we want to make the daring hypothesis that there are some gestalt

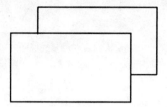

Figure 9.1: An example for a gestalt phenomenon possibly involving spatial persistence.

phenomena that can be described by postulating that the human perception actually applies a certain form of spatial persistence. As an example, consider figure 9.1, where most people would agree that the right—well—rectangle *is* a rectangle although you just see four lines.

Our approach to spatial reasoning cannot handle such persistence. However, like there was a way from Allen's temporal relations to practical systems for time map management [Dean and McDermott, 1987], there should be a way from Allen-type spatial relations to space map managers, which might be of considerable practical use in applications involving spatial reasoning. But this is further research.

Let us now consider how our approach to spatial reasoning fits into the framework of spatial reasoning as such. From a more general point of view, the various approaches to spatial reasoning may be categorized according to the kind of representation they use: intrinsic, extrinsic, or deictic representations (cf. [Retz-Schmidt, 1988]). A deictic representation applies an external reference frame to relate the objects to each other. Such a reference frame may be given by Cartesian coordinates, as suggested in chapter 2. In contrast to this, intrinsic and extrinsic representations are based on the directions of the objects. The direction of an object may be given either intrinsically as an immanent part of the object itself (e.g., each car has a front and a back) or extrinsically as a feature imposed on the object by, for example, movement (e.g., if a car is setting back, the extrinsic direction is the reverse of the intrinsic one). An example for an intrinsic/extrinsic representation is the one suggested in [Mukerjee and Joe, 1990] for expressing information on direction.

Especially in the case of deictic representations, the choice of the underlying reference frame may be crucial. In all chapters of this text, we have used Cartesian coordinates, which yield correct results of the reasoning process if dealing with cubic objects (or circumscribing cubes of objects) adjusted in parallel to the axes in space. However, the world may be more complicated. As an example in 2D space, consider the situation in figure 9.2. The circle overlaps the triangle in x direction, and it includes the triangle in y direction in our model. However, this may be counterintuitive, since the triangle and the circle do not occupy common space. A solution here would be to use non-orthogonal coordinates, for example, polar coordinates.

Note that the problem of choosing an adequate coordinate system is no issue in the area of temporal reasoning: time knows only one axis along which it is moving. Only when

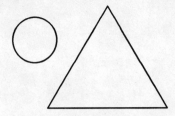

Figure 9.2: A situation whose description in Cartesian coordinates may yield wrong results.

trying to adapt temporal reasoning techniques to spatial descriptions, we are confronted with the problem of selecting a coordinate system that is appropriate for the task we want to solve.

To summarize, our approach is Allen-type reasoning applied to multi-dimensional spatial descriptions. Thus, it is suitable if

- deictic representations are adequate to model the given problem,

- relationships between objects are to be described, and

- Cartesian coordinates are appropriate as reference frame.

If these prerequisits are not fulfilled by some particular application area, one should use other genuine spatial reasoning approaches; alternatively, one may try to look at other approaches in the area of temporal reasoning to see whether they can be transferred to spatial reasoning more successfully. If all this fails, there is still the hope that basic techniques such as dynamic constraints may help to solve the problem from bottom up. This text could be a guideline for this enterprise.

Figure 6.x ...

Bibliography

[Aarts and Korst, 1989] E. Aarts and J. Korst. *Simulated Annealing and Boltzmann Machines*. John Wiley & Sons, Cichester, England, 1989.

[Adorf and Johnston, 1990] H.M. Adorf and M.D. Johnston. A discrete stochastic neural network algorithm for constraint satisfaction problems. In *Proc. IJCNN-90*, pages 917–924, San Diego, California, 1990.

[Allen, 1983] J.F. Allen. Maintaining knowledge about temporal intervals. *Communications of the ACM*, 26:832–843, 1983.

[Bessière, 1991] C. Bessière. Arc-consistency in dynamic constraint satisfaction problems. In *Proc. of the 10 th AAAI*, pages 221–226, Anaheim, California, 1991.

[Bibel, 1988] W. Bibel. Constraint satisfaction from a deductive viewpoint. *J. Artificial Intelligence*, 35:401–413, 1988.

[Bolz and Wittur, 1990] D. Bolz and K. Wittur. Die Umsetzung deklarativer Beschreibungen von Graphiken durch Simulated Annealing. In P. Wißkirchen K. Kansy, editor, *Proc. GI-Fachgespräch Graphik und KI*, pages 68–77, Berlin, Germany, 1990. Springer.

[Borning et al., 1987] A. Borning, R. Duisberg, B. Freeman-Benson, A. Kramer, and M. Woolf. Constraint hierarchies. In *Proc. 1987 ACM Conference on Object-Oriented Programming Systems, Languages and Applications*, pages 48–60, Orlando, Florida, 1987.

[Borning, 1981] A. Borning. The programming language aspects of ThingLab, a constraint-oriented simulation laboratory. *ACM Transactions on Programming Languages and Systems*, 3:353–387, 1981.

[Brewka et al., 1992] G. Brewka, H.W. Guesgen, and J. Hertzberg. Constraint relaxation and nonmonotonic reasoning. Technical Report TR-92-002, ICSI, Berkeley, California, 1992.

[Brewka, 1989] G. Brewka. Preferred subtheories: An extended logical framework for default reasoning. In *Proc. of the 11 th IJCAI*, pages 1043–1048, Detroit, Michigan, 1989.

[Brewka, 1991] G. Brewka. *Nonmonotonic Reasoning: Logical Foundations of Commonsense*. Cambridge University Press, Cambridge, England, 1991.

[Bürckert, 1991] H.-J. Bürckert. *A Resolution Principle for a Logic with Restricted Quantifiers*. Lecture Notes in Artificial Intelligence 568. Springer, Berlin, Germany, 1991.

[Cooper and Swain, 1988] P.R. Cooper and M.J. Swain. Parallelism and domain dependence in constraint satisfaction. Technical Report 255, University of Rochester, Computer Science Department, Rochester, New York, 1988.

[Cooper, 1989] P.R. Cooper. Parallel object recognition from structure (the tinkertoy project). Technical Report 301, University of Rochester, Computer Science Department, Rochester, New York, 1989.

[Davis, 1984] R. Davis. Diagnostic reasoning based on structure and behavior. *J. Artificial Intelligence*, 24:347–410, 1984.

[Davis, 1987] E. Davis. Constraint propagation with interval labels. *J. Artificial Intelligence*, 32:281–331, 1987.

[Davis, 1989] E. Davis. Solutions to a paradox of perception with limited acuity. In *Proc. of the 1 st KR*, pages 79–82, Toronto, Canada, 1989.

[de Kleer and Brown, 1984] J. de Kleer and J.S. Brown. A qualitative physics based on confluences. *J. Artificial Intelligence*, 24:7–84, 1984.

[de Kleer and Williams, 1986] J. de Kleer and B.C. Williams. Diagnosing multiple faults. In *Proc. of the 5 th AAAI*, pages 132–139, Philadelphia, Pennsylvania, 1986.

[de Kleer, 1989] J. de Kleer. A comparison of ATMS and CSP techniques. In *Proc. of the 11 th IJCAI*, pages 290–296, Detroit, Michigan, 1989.

[Dean and McDermott, 1987] T.L. Dean and D.V. McDermott. Temporal data base management. *J. Artificial Intelligence*, 32:1–55, 1987.

[Dechter and Dechter, 1988] R. Dechter and A. Dechter. Belief maintenance in dynamic constraint networks. In *Proc. of the 8 th AAAI*, pages 37–42, St. Paul, Minnesota, 1988.

[Dechter and Meiri, 1989] R. Dechter and I. Meiri. Experimental evaluation of preprocessing techniques in constraint satisfaction problems. In *Proc. of the 11 th IJCAI*, pages 271–277, Detroit, Michigan, 1989.

[Dechter and Pearl, 1985] R. Dechter and J. Pearl. The anatomy of easy problems: A constraint-satisfaction formulation. In *Proc. of the 9 th IJCAI*, pages 1066–1072, Los Angeles, California, 1985.

[Dechter and Pearl, 1987] R. Dechter and J. Pearl. Network-based heuristics for constraint-satisfaction problems. *J. Artificial Intelligence*, 34:1–38, 1987.

[Dechter and Pearl, 1988] R. Dechter and J. Pearl. Tree-clustering schemes for constraint-processing. In *Proc. of the 8 th AAAI*, pages 150–154, St. Paul, Minnesota, 1988.

[Dechter et al., 1991] R. Dechter, I. Meiri, and J. Pearl. Temporal constraint networks. *J. Artificial Intelligence*, 49:61–95, 1991.

[Dechter, 1990] R. Dechter. Enhancement schemes for constraint processing: Backjumbing, learning, and cutset decomposition. *J. Artificial Intelligence*, 41:273–312, 1990.

[Descotte and Latombe, 1985] Y. Descotte and J.C. Latombe. Making compromises among antagonist constraints in a planner. *J. Artificial Intelligence*, 27:183–217, 1985.

[Dincbas et al., 1987] M. Dincbas, H. Simonis, and P. van Hentenryck. Extending equation solving and constraint handling in logic programming. In *Proc. Colloquium on Resolution of Equations in Algebraic Structures*, MCC, Austin, Texas, 1987.

[Egenhofer, 1991] M.J. Egenhofer. Reasoning about binary topological relations. In *Proc. SSD-91*, pages 143–160, Zurich, Switzerland, 1991. Lecture Notes in Computer Science, Springer, Berlin, Germany.

[Feldman and Ballard, 1982] J.A. Feldman and D.H. Ballard. Connectionist models and their properties. *J. Cognitive Science*, 6:201–254, 1982.

[Fendler and Wichlacz, 1987] M. Fendler and R. Wichlacz. Symbolische Constraint-Propagierung auf Netzwerken, Entwurf und Implementierung. KI-Labor Bericht 15, Universität Saarbrücken, Saarbrücken, Germany, 1987.

[Fidelak and Guesgen, 1988] M. Fidelak and H.W. Guesgen. Improving local constraint propagation. TEX-B Memo 31-88, GMD, St. Augustin, Germany, 1988.

[Fidelak et al., 1989] M. Fidelak, H.W. Guesgen, and H. Voss. Temporal aspects in constrained-based reasoning. In *Proc. IEA/AIE-89*, pages 794–802, Tullahoma, Tennessee, 1989.

[Fikes, 1970] R.E. Fikes. REF-ARF: A system for solving problems stated as procedures. *J. Artificial Intelligence*, 1:27–120, 1970.

[Forbus, 1984] K.D. Forbus. Qualitative process theory. *J. Artificial Intelligence*, 24:85–168, 1984.

[Fox *et al.*, 1982] M.S. Fox, B. Allen, and G. Strohm. Job-shop scheduling: An investigation in constraint-directed reasoning. In *Proc. of the 2nd AAAI*, pages 155–158, Pittsburgh, Pennsylvania, 1982.

[Freeman-Benson *et al.*, 1990] B.N. Freeman-Benson, J. Maloney, and A. Borning. An incremental constraint solver. *Communications of the ACM*, 33:54–63, 1990.

[Freksa, 1990] C. Freksa. Qualitative spatial reasoning. In *Proc. Workshop RAUM*, pages 21–36, Koblenz, Germany, 1990. Universität Koblenz-Landau, Fachberichte Informatik No. 9/90.

[Freuder, 1978] E.C. Freuder. Synthesizing constraint expressions. *Communications of the ACM*, 21:958–966, 1978.

[Freuder, 1982] E.C. Freuder. A sufficient condition for backtrack-free search. *Journal of the ACM*, 29:24–32, 1982.

[Freuder, 1989] E.C. Freuder. Partial constraint satisfaction. In *Proc. of the 11th IJCAI*, pages 278–283, Detroit, Michigan, 1989.

[Gaschnig, 1979] J. Gaschnig. Performance measurement and analysis of certain search algorithms. Technical Report CMU-CS-79-124, Department of Computer Science, Carnegie Mellon University, Pittsburgh, Pennsylvania, 1979.

[Geffner and Pearl, 1987] H. Geffner and J. Pearl. An improved constraint-propagation algorithm for diagnosis. In *Proc. of the 10th IJCAI*, pages 1105–1111, Milan, Italy, 1987.

[Gosling, 1983] J. Gosling. Algebraic constraints. Technical Report CMU-CS-83-132, Department of Computer Science, Carnegie Mellon University, Pittsburgh, Pennsylvania, 1983.

[Gu *et al.*, 1987] J. Gu, W. Wang, and T.C. Henderson. A parallel architecture for discrete relaxation algorithm. *IEEE Transactions on Pattern Analysis and Machine Intelligence*, 9:816–831, 1987.

[Guesgen and Hertzberg, 1988] H.W. Guesgen and J. Hertzberg. Some fundamental properties of local constraint propagation. *J. Artificial Intelligence*, 36:237–247, 1988.

[Guesgen and Ladkin, 1990] H.W. Guesgen and P. Ladkin. An algebraic approach to general boolean constraint problems. Technical Report TR-90-008, ICSI, Berkeley, California, 1990.

[Guesgen *et al.*, 1987] H.W. Guesgen, U. Junker, and A. Voss. Constraints in a hybrid knowledge representation system. In *Proc. of the 10th IJCAI*, pages 30–33, Milan, Italy, 1987.

[Guesgen, 1989a] H.W. Guesgen. *CONSAT: A System for Constraint Satisfaction*. Research Notes in Artificial Intelligence. Morgan Kaufmann, San Mateo, California, 1989.

[Guesgen, 1989b] H.W. Guesgen. Four-dimensional reasoning. In *Proc. IASTED International Conference on Expert Systems: Theory and Applications*, pages 99–103, Long Beach, California, 1989.

[Guesgen, 1989c] H.W. Guesgen. A universal constraint programming language. In *Proc. of the 11th IJCAI*, pages 60–65, Detroit, Michigan, 1989.

[Guesgen, 1991] H.W. Guesgen. Connectionist networks for constraint satisfaction. In *Working Notes 1991 AAAI Spring Symposium on Constraint-Based Reasoning*, pages 182–190, Stanford, California, 1991.

[Haralick and Elliott, 1980] R.M. Haralick and G.L. Elliott. Increasing tree search efficiency for constraint satisfaction problems. *J. Artificial Intelligence*, 14:263–313, 1980.

[Haralick and Shapiro, 1979] R.M. Haralick and L. Shapiro. The consistent labeling problem: Part 1. *IEEE Transactions on Pattern Analysis and Machine Intelligence*, 1:173–184, 1979.

[Harris, 1986] D.R. Harris. A hybrid structured object and constraint representation language. In *Proc. of the 5th AAAI*, pages 986–990, Philadelphia, Pennsylvania, 1986.

[Hayes, 1979] P.J. Hayes. The naive physics manifesto. In D. Michie, editor, *Expert Systems in the Micro-Electronic Age*, pages 242–270. Edinburgh University Press, 1979.

[Hernandez, 1990] D. Hernandez. Using comparative relations to represent spatial knowledge. In *Proc. Workshop RAUM*, pages 69–80, Koblenz, Germany, 1990. Universität Koblenz-Landau, Fachberichte Informatik No. 9/90.

[Hertzberg *et al.*, 1988] J. Hertzberg, H.W. Guesgen, and H. Voss A. Voss, M. Fidelak. Relaxing constraint networks to resolve inconsistencies. In *Proc. of the 12 th GWAI*, pages 61–65, Eringerfeld, Germany, 1988.

[Hinton, 1977] G.E. Hinton. *Relaxation and its Role in Vision*. PhD thesis, University of Edinburgh, Edinburgh, Scotland, 1977.

[Ho *et al.*, 1991] K. Ho, P.N. Hilfinger, and H.W. Guesgen. Global constraint satisfaction using parallel relaxation. Unpublished paper, July 1991.

[Horn, 1986] B.K.P. Horn. *Polyhedral Objects*. MIT Press, Cambridge, Massachusetts, 1986.

[Hummel and Zucker, 1983] R.A. Hummel and S.W. Zucker. On the foundations of relaxation labeling processes. *IEEE Transactions on Pattern Analysis and Machine Intelligence*, 5:267–287, 1983.

[Jaffar and Lassez, 1987] J. Jaffar and J.L. Lassez. Constraint logic programming. In *Conference Record of the 14 th Annual ACM Symposium on Principles of Programming Languages*, pages 111–119, Munich, Germany, 1987.

[Johnston and Adorf, 1989] M.D. Johnston and H.M. Adorf. Learning in stochastic neural networks for constraint satisfaction problems. In G. Rodriguez and H. Seraij, editors, *Proc. NASA Conference on Space Telerobotics*, pages 367–376. JPL Publ., 1989.

[Kak, 1988] A. Kak. Spatial reasoning. *AI Magazine*, 9(2):23, 1988.

[Kasif, 1986] S. Kasif. On the parallel complexity of some constraint satisfaction problems. In *Proc. of the 5 th AAAI*, pages 349–353, Philadelphia, Pennsylvania, 1986.

[Kasif, 1989] S. Kasif. Parallel solutions to constraint satisfaction problems. In *Proc. of the 1 st KR*, pages 180–188, Toronto, Canada, 1989.

[Kautz and Ladkin, 1991] H.A. Kautz and P.B. Ladkin. Integrating metric and qualitative temporal reasoning. In *Proc. of the 10 th AAAI*, pages 241–246, Anaheim, California, 1991.

[Kitchen and Rosenfeld, 1979] L. Kitchen and A. Rosenfeld. Discrete relaxation for matching relational structures. *IEEE Transactions on Systems, Man, and Cybernetics*, 9:869–874, 1979.

[Komen, 1989] J.A.G.M. Komen. Localizing temporal constraint propagation. In *Proc. of the 1 st KR*, pages 198–202, Toronto, Canada, 1989.

[Kuipers, 1977] B. Kuipers. Modeling spatial knowledge. In *Proc. of the 5 th IJCAI*, pages 292–298, Cambridge, Massachusetts, 1977.

[Kuipers, 1984] B. Kuipers. Commonsense reasoning about causality: Deriving behavior from structure. *J. Artificial Intelligence*, 24:169–204, 1984.

[Ladkin, 1988] P.B. Ladkin. Satisfying first-order constraints about time intervals. In *Proc. of the 8 th AAAI*, pages 512–517, St. Paul, Minnesota, 1988.

[Ladkin, 1989] P.B. Ladkin. Metric constraint satisfaction with intervals. Technical Report TR-89-038, ICSI, Berkeley, California, 1989.

[Lange and Dyer, 1989] T.E. Lange and M.G. Dyer. High-level inferencing in a connectionist network. Technical Report UCLA-AI-89-12, University of California, Los Angeles, California, 1989.

[Lischka and Guesgen, 1986] C. Lischka and H.W. Guesgen. $M \vee S \mid C$: A constrained-based approach to musical knowledge representation. In *Proc. ICMC-86*, pages 227–229, The Hague, The Netherlands, 1986.

[Mackworth and Freuder, 1985] A.K. Mackworth and E.C. Freuder. The complexity of some polynomial network consistency algorithms for constraint satisfaction problems. *J. Artificial Intelligence*, 25:65–74, 1985.

[Mackworth *et al.*, 1985] A.K. Mackworth, J.A. Mulder, and W.S. Havens. Hierarchical arc consistency: Exploiting structured domains in constraint satisfaction problems. *J. Computational Intelligence*, 1:118–126, 1985.

[Mackworth, 1977] A.K. Mackworth. Consistency in networks of relations. *J. Artificial Intelligence*, 8:99–118, 1977.

[Maddux, 1989] R.D. Maddux. Some algebras and algorithms for reasoning about time and space. Internal paper, Department of Mathematics, Iowa State University, Ames, Iowa, 1989.

[Maes, 1987] P. Maes. Computational reflection. Technical Report 87.2, Artificial Intelligence Laboratory, Vrije Universiteit Brussel, Brussel, Belgium, 1987.

[Malik and Binford, 1983] J. Malik and T.O. Binford. Reasoning in time and space. In *Proc. of the 8 th IJCAI*, pages 343–345, Karlsruhe, Germany, 1983.

[Meiri, 1991] I. Meiri. Combining qualitative and quantitative constraints in temporal reasoning. In *Proc. of the 10 th AAAI*, pages 260–267, Anaheim, California, 1991.

[Minton *et al.*, 1990] S. Minton, M.D. Johnston, A.B. Philips, and P. Laird. Solving large-scale constraint satisfaction and scheduling problems using a heuristic repair method. In *Proc. of the 9 th AAAI*, pages 17–24, Boston, Massachusetts, 1990.

[Mohr and Henderson, 1986] R. Mohr and T.C. Henderson. Arc and path consistency revisited. *J. Artificial Intelligence*, 28:225–233, 1986.

[Montanari and Rossi, 1991] U. Montanari and F. Rossi. Constraint relaxation may be perfect. *J. Artificial Intelligence*, 48:143–170, 1991.

[Montanari, 1974] U. Montanari. Networks of constraints: Fundamental properties and applications to picture processing. *Information Sciences*, 7:95–132, 1974.

[Mukerjee and Joe, 1990] A. Mukerjee and G. Joe. A qualitative model for space. In *Proc. of the 9 th AAAI*, pages 721–727, Boston, Massachusetts, 1990.

[Nadel, 1986] B.A. Nadel. The general constraint labeling (or constraint satisfaction) problem. Technical Report DCS-TR-170, Department of Computer Science, Rutgers University, New Brunswick, New Jersey, 1986.

[Pinkas, 1991] G. Pinkas. Propositional non-monotonic reasoning and inconsistency in symmetric neural networks. In *Proc. of the 12 th IJCAI*, pages 525–530, Sidney, Australia, 1991.

[Poole, 1988] D. Poole. A logical framework for default reasoning. *J. Artificial Intelligence*, 36:27–47, 1988.

[Purdom, 1983] P.W. Purdom. Search rearrangement backtracking and polynomial average time. *J. Artificial Intelligence*, 21:117–133, 1983.

[Reinfrank, 1984] M. Reinfrank. Distributed constraint propagation: A case study. Memo SEKI-84-07, Universität Kaiserslautern, Kaiserslautern, Germany, 1984.

[Reinfrank, 1985] M. Reinfrank. Scenelab: Scene labelling by a society of agents, a distributed constraint propagation system. Memo SEKI-85-06, Universität Kaiserslautern, Kaiserslautern, Germany, 1985.

[Retz-Schmidt, 1988] G. Retz-Schmidt. Various views on spatial prepositions. *AI Magazine*, 9(2):95–105, 1988.

[Rosenfeld *et al.*, 1976] A. Rosenfeld, R.A. Hummel, and S.W. Zucker. Scene labeling by relaxation operations. *IEEE Transactions on Systems, Man, and Cybernetics*, 6:420–433, 1976.

[Rosenfeld, 1975] A. Rosenfeld. Networks of automata: Some applications. *IEEE Transactions on Systems, Man, and Cybernetics*, 5:380–383, 1975.

[Samal and Henderson, 1987] A. Samal and T.C. Henderson. Parallel consistent labeling algorithms. *International Journal of Parallel Programming*, 16:341–364, 1987.

[Shapiro, 1987] S.C. Shapiro, editor. *Encyclopedia of Artificial Intelligence.* John Wiley & Sons, Chichester, England, 1987.

[Shastri, 1989] L. Shastri. Connectionism, knowledge representation, and effective reasoning. In *Proc. Internationaler GI-Kongreß Wissensbasierte Systeme*, pages 186–195, Munich, Germany, 1989.

[Shoham and McDermott, 1988] Y. Shoham and D.V. McDermott. Problems in formal temporal reasoning. *J. Artificial Intelligence*, 36:49–61, 1988.

[Stallman and Sussman, 1977] R.M. Stallman and G.J. Sussman. Forward reasoning and dependency-directed backtracking in a system for computer-aided circuit analysis. *J. Artificial Intelligence*, 9:135–196, 1977.

[Steele, 1980] G.L. Steele. The definition and implementation of a computer programming language based on constraints. Technical Report AI-TR-595, Massachusetts Institute of Technology, Cambridge, Massachusetts, 1980.

[Steels, 1980] L. Steels. The constraint machine. AI Memo 1, Schlumberger-Doll Research Lab, Ridgefield, Connecticut, 1980.

[Steels, 1984] L. Steels. Object-oriented knowledge representation in KRS. In *Proc. of the 6 th ECAI*, pages 333–336, Pisa, Italy, 1984.

[Steels, 1985] L. Steels. Constraints as consultants. In L. Steels and J.A. Campbell, editors, *Progress in Artificial Intelligence*, pages 146–165. John Wiley & Sons, Chichester, England, 1985.

[Stefik, 1981] M. Stefik. Planning with constraints (MOLGEN: Part 1). *J. Artificial Intelligence*, 16:111–140, 1981.

[Stone and Stone, 1986] H.S. Stone and J.M. Stone. Efficient search techniques: An empirical study of the n-queens problem. Technical Report RC 12057 (#54343), IBM T.J. Watson Research Center, Yorktown Heights, New York, 1986.

[Sussman and Steele, 1980] G.J. Sussman and G.L. Steele. Constraints: A language for expressing almost-hierarchical descriptions. *J. Artificial Intelligence*, 14:1–39, 1980.

[Tsang and Howarth, 1991] E. Tsang and R. Howarth. Scheduling in both space and time. In *Proc. 11th International Workshop on Expert Systems and their Applications, vol.3*, pages 361–372, 1991.

[van Hentenryck and Dincbas, 1986] P. van Hentenryck and M. Dincbas. Domains in logic programming. In *Proc. of the 5 th AAAI*, pages 759–765, Philadelphia, Pennsylvania, 1986.

[van Hentenryck, 1987] P. van Hentenryck. A theoretical framework for consistency techniques in logic programming. In *Proc. of the 10 th IJCAI*, pages 2–8, Milan, Italy, 1987.

[van Hentenryck, 1989] P. van Hentenryck. *Constraint Satisfaction in Logic Programming.* MIT Press, Cambridge, Massachusetts, 1989.

[Voß and Voß, 1987] A. Voß and H. Voß. Formalizing local constraint propagation methods. In *Proc. of the 5 th KIFS*, pages 218–260, Günne, Germany, 1987.

[Voß et al., 1987] A. Voß, W. Karbach, U. Drouven, B. Bartsch-Spoerl, and B. Bredeweg. Reflection and competent problem solving. In *Proc. of the 15 th GWAI*, pages 206–215, Bonn, Germany, 1987.

[Waltz, 1972] D.L. Waltz. Generating semantic descriptions from drawings of scenes with shadows. Technical Report AI-TR-271, Massachusetts Institute of Technology, Cambridge, Massachusetts, 1972.

[Weld and de Kleer, 1990] D.S. Weld and J. de Kleer, editors. *Readings in Qualitative Reasoning about Physical Systems.* Morgan Kaufmann, San Mateo, California, 1990.

[Williams, 1986] B.C. Williams. Doing time: Putting qualitative reasoning on firmer ground. In *Proc. of the 5 th AAAI*, pages 105–112, Philadelphia, Pennsylvania, 1986.

[Zabih and McAllester, 1988] R. Zabih and D. McAllester. A rearrangement search strategy for determining propositional satisfiability. In *Proc. of the 8 th AAAI*, pages 155–160, St. Paul, Minnesota, 1988.

Index

The following conventions are applied in this index: Page numbers are typesetted in *italics* when they represent introductory occurences of concepts. If a page number refers to the definition of a concept, **bold** is used as font. All other references are typesetted in plain font.

Lecture Notes in Artificial Intelligence (LNAI)

Lecture Notes in Computer Science